Roman Incense

Roman Incense

Journey to God

David Bellusci

Leonine Publishers
Phoenix, Arizona

Copyright © 2019 David Bellusci

All rights reserved. No part of this book may be reproduced or transmitted in any form or by any means, electronic or mechanical, including photocopying, recording, or by any information storage or retrieval system now existing or to be invented, without written permission from the respective copyright holder(s), except for the inclusion of brief quotations in a review.

Published by
Leonine Publishers LLC
Phoenix, Arizona, USA

ISBN-13: 978-1-942190-54-7

Library of Congress Control Number: 2019912456

Visit us online at www.leoninepublishers.com
For more information: info@leoninepublishers.com

*In memory of my mother, Rosa Montagano Bellusci
and my father, Nicola Bellusci*

Therefore, I urge you, brothers and sisters,
in view of God's mercy,
to offer your bodies as a living sacrifice,
holy and pleasing to God—
this is your true and proper worship.

Romans 12:1

Contents

Foreword xiii
Preface xx

Part 1: French Novitiate – I*

Doctor of Divine Love 2
Prayer of a Novice 3
Roman Martyrs 5
Vigils on a Hill 6
Silence of Monks 7
November Consecration 8
Toucher (To Touch) 9
I Desire 10
Word/s 12
Heights of Montmorin 13
His Eyes Close 14
Discernment 15
Loyola Chapel, Montreal 16
Lovesong* 17
Abandonment 18
June 16, 2002 19

Part 2: French Novitiate – II

St. Dominic's Ascent 22
Thanksgiving= 24
All Saints 25
Holy Souls 26
Nuns in White Habits 27
December 24th 28

University of Toronto, Twenty Years Later 29
Joseph in the Pews 31
Berthierville Prayers 33
On Being a Monk 34
Silent Wait 35
Brother Silence 36
Death of Priests 38
Buckled Shoe 40
St. Joseph: Prayer of a Novice 42

Part 3: Sea Salt and Oil Lamps
Cassiar Street* 46
Papa's Chair* 48
Sister Mary 50
Angel Voices 52
Picture of a Shepherd Boy 53
My Nephew's Canvas 54
Emily in Carmel 55
Consecrated Virgin 56
Rue Saint-Sulpice 58
Saint Michael's Cafeteria 59
Office Hours 60
Teachings of a Mystic 62
Sacred Space 63
Tombstones 64
Widow in the Pew 65
Caribbean Outpost 67
Plaza Bolivar 69
Sopa de Queso (Cheese Soup) 70
Monsoon Prayers 71
Goan Intersections 73
Nagpur Candles 74

Paris Kneels 75
Turtle and Elephant 76
Hills of Umbria 77
"Vision of St. Dominic" 79
My Tower 80
Facing East 82
Indie Music 84
Roman Sun 86

Part 4: Graeco-Roman Meditations
Interior Fortress 88
Piazza Navona: Northern Fountain – Late October 89
Piazza Navona: Center Fountain – Late November 90
Piazza Navona: Southern Fountain – Late December . . . 91
Voyage of the Soul 92
Narcissus 93
Piazza del Pasquino 94
Fuoco Rubato (Stolen Fire) 95
Gallerie Alberto Sordi (Colonna) 96
Slaughter of the Innocents 97
Parmigianino – Barocci* 98

Part 5: Holy Year
Silent Words on Sacred Cloth 100
Prayer Before Salus Populi Romani* 102
Visitors at the Basilica 104
Third Week of September 106
San Martino ai Monti 107
Sacristy Prayers 108
Sante Domenicane (Dominican Saints) 109
Joy of the Cloister 110
Reliquaries of Conjugal Love 111
Roman Cemetery 112

Rome: All Saints. 113
Ponte Sant'Angelo by Night 114
First Week of Advent 115
Our Lady of Loreto 116
Christmas Colors in Rome. 117
Nativity in Rome 118
Opening the Holy Door. 119
Prayer of a Confessor 121
Confession 122
Adolescent Cry. 123
Santa Maria della Vittoria: Chapter 29* 124
Metaphysics of Divine Love 125
Condolences in Lucera. 127
Byzantine Tower* 130
Madonna della Sanità (Our Lady of Health)* 131
Bolsena's Miracle 132
Joy in Bologna 134
Finnish Footsteps in Rome. 136
Closure of a Roman Summer 138

Part 6: Blessed Pier Giorgio Collection

Prayers on a Holy Mountain 142
Silence of Oropa. 144
Hills of Beauty 145
My Oropa Cell. 146
Below Mount Mucrone 147
Kneeling Before You. 148
Lunch by the "Ruscello"* 149
April 6th: Praying with Blessed Pier Giorgio 150
Breath of Time (Night before leaving Oropa) 152

Part 7: Pilgrim Gates

Sacred Soil 156

Nuns of Rweza	157
At Carmel	159
August 2009 — First Masses	161
Poem for Our Blessed Lady*	163
Grotto in Shepherd's Field*	164
Clothed in White	165
Roman Setting	167
Capes and Hoods	168
Cause of Our Joy – "La Gritería"*	169
"La Purísima" (Most Pure One)	170
Nicaragua Nuns	171
My Fifth Year	172
Morning in Prague	173
Finding Warsaw	174
Kneeling in Częstochowa*	175
Mother of Auschwitz	177
Priest at a Death Camp	178
White Wine with Anne	179
Jesus Holds a Porcelain Wicker Basket	181
April in Galilee	182
On the Sea of Galilee	183
Our Lady of Altötting	184
Solitudine (Solitude)*	186
Saluti da Roma* — (Greetings from Rome)	187
La Vita è Bella — "Life is Beautiful"	188
Wedding Colors	189
Blessing of Autumn Classes	190
Mary Mother of God, 2018	191
Feast of the Presentation at the Benedictine Monastery	195
Mountain Nuns	196
First Communion	197

Foreword

Introduction

When I first met David Bellusci, he was wearing his white Dominican habit. He had submitted his poem for the 22nd edition of the Cala Petralana Poetry of which I am the co-founder, president, and organizer. Bellusci's poem, "*Fuoco Rubato*" ("Stolen Fire"), was well-received by the jury and won the Special Jury's Prize of 2017. In "Stolen Fire," Bellusci spoke of Zeus, Tantalus, Pegasus, and Prometheus the Titan who "stole the fire" from Zeus and gave it to humanity—the world of classic mythology.

After reading his 142 poems, I can see how very dear to Bellusci are:

- the individual in his various expressions/feelings
- space-time relations
- nature/the metaphysical
- theology/mysticism (The Holy Trinity, the Virgin Mary, and the saints, especially Dominic, Joseph, Thérèse of Lisieux, and Pier Giorgio Frassati)

The collection is divided into seven parts, from "French Novitiate" to "Pilgrim Gates," with intervening sections titled "French Novitiate 2," "Sea Salt and Oil Lamps," "Graeco-Roman Meditations," "Holy Year," and "Blessed Pier Giorgio Collection."

The poems were written between 1998 and 2018, having been inspired by places visited and experiences had by the author. They draw from the reservoir of his memory and mirror his innermost thoughts and hopes. He loves journeys as well as his life as a Dominican friar. Bellusci, to me, appears to assume the role of the first disciples, who with Jesus were *viatores*, "on the way," the same to whom Jesus said, *Euntes ergo docete omnes gentes…* (Mt. 28:19).

Bellusci's language is metaphysical, pure, rich in expression, lyrical, and deeply meditational.

Man in his various expressions and appearances

For Bellusci, man is synonymous with energy, life, feelings, emotions, love—in one word: heart. It is not by chance that "heart" is frequently referred to in his poems, found within such words as "life," "father," "mother," "faith," "hope," "family."

"Oh, Mother of hope…I feel alone, my Mother…" ("Prayer of a Novice.") Also, "Oh, Thérèse! Lead me to Jesus my life…" ("Doctor of Divine Love.") And perhaps in "Québec ignored the heroic saint. / Friars and family remember…" ("Death of Priests.")

Poetry is like a dream that says and yet does not say, but gives the impression of imminent revelation. In this time of nihilism and in our consumer society, good poetry is an effective antidote. Such a journey enriches the poet in the creation of ideas, images, words; we must not forget that the word "poem" derives from the Greek *poieo*, "I make, I create." In "My Nephew's Canvas," Bellusci writes, "…imagination guided, senses feel / emotions painted / meditating the theme / object and subject unite / the transcendent…"

According to the Orphic doctrine, man is the son of Earth and of starry Heaven. Out of myth we can say that he is moulded from materiality and divinity. We can say, too, that man is truly a person when he becomes conscious of this double nature. This may happen (as in Bellusci) through a self-examination in the journey of life, confronting the crosses which contemporary culture obliges the person to carry. In other words, the individual of today is situated between two different impulses: the need of belonging and the need to seek innovation. He shuts himself up, in the first case, and looks for something capable of giving protection in the second—knowledge and fulfilment, respectively.

Not all people think that this "something" is simply the Lord! *He* is the model for the person! He is the only one who gives faith, hope, and charity! Not only thanks to His Resurrection, the individual, each individual, will have his own resurrection, joining his destiny to God in eternal life. But Love is essential. Saint Thérèse of Lisieux wrote: "Only Love makes us appreciated by God: Love! He doesn't need our works, but exclusively our love…" And our poet says, "Oh, Thérèse! Show me the way to divine love." ("Doctor of Divine Love.")

Let us walk, then, in this way, renewed by Faith and Love.

Nature and Metaphysics

Bellusci's poetry follows its course in a meandering route; he observes nature, but he aims high, from the sublime to Transcendence. The poet, "our poet," is, in a sense, one of God's Minister's of religion: the reign of the Spirit reaches the incommensurable. And the poet for a short time forgets the world of things.

His "room" in the pages of his journey—youth, family, friends, studies, novitiate—allows him to live in a climate of faith, in relation to his community and the Lord; and, ultimately, to attain and experience the theological meaning of being human in relation to God, the God of the Christian faith. To reference G. K. Chesterton in his book *The Everlasting Man*: "The Catholic faith is a reconciliation, because in the realisation between mythology and philosophy…it is true history… a history both human and divine…" Religion moves along the horizontal parameter of personality because going from sharing to Being involves communication and Communion with God in a universal bond. Through religion, each person expresses the capability of transcending himself because he is a religious being.

But what is the human person? What is the secret of a happy human life? What do our relationships, our experiences, our memories mean? Can we, without looking at Divine reality, reflect with integrity the phenomenon of human experience with all its richness? Authoritative explanations were offered by Pope Benedict XVI in 2005, on the Solemnity of the Assumption in his homily at the Parish Church of Castel Gandolfo:

"Previously, it was thought and believed that by setting God aside and being autonomous, following only our own ideas and inclinations, we would truly be free to do whatever we liked without anyone being able to give us orders. But when God disappears, men and women do not become greater; indeed, they lose the divine dignity, their faces lose God's splendour. In the end, they turn out to be merely products of a blind evolution and, as such, can be used and abused. This is precisely what the experience of our epoch has confirmed for us."

Bellusci writes, "I found my way as a mission teacher / my father a soldier swept away. / Stories of your glory, / silent treasures, ancient secrets. / …My father praised you—/ and dreamed about you…" ("Sacred Soil," Part 7).

Philosophy, Theology, Mysticism

In his *Stromata*, Clement of Alexandria (2nd century A.D.) considered the Christian religion as a philosophy. Ancient philosophers sought through their own philosophy to attain a nobler and holier life; this was also the aim of Christianity. The difference between the two is that the Greek philosophers had only glimpses of the truth—they attained only fragments of the truth—while Christianity revealed, in Christ, the absolute and perfect truth.

"Philosophy," Clement wrote, "is an exercise towards knowledge, that is, science towards human and divine things…The Logos is the new chant that puts harmoniously in order all creation."

What does our poet say? Let's read an excerpt of Bellusci's poem "Prayer Before *Salus Populi Romani*":

> "...I desire Courage to proclaim and defend
> the truths the Catholic Church teaches,
> from Scriptures, Tradition,
> the Supreme Law of God, Natural Law.
> That criticism, persecution, slander
> will not weaken me, but fortify me.
> Let humility be my guide, to rid me
> of pride, Satan's cunning, twisted
> reasoning. Let Humility manifest
> how dependent I am on Divine Grace,
> that keeps my heart beating..."

When our soul is full of Jesus, our soul is full of love. Love, Bellusci writes, is the most powerful way to be loved: "Guide me, Saint Joseph: / to perfect love / so I may be with Jesus / True Love." ("St. Joseph: Prayer of a Novice"). From then on, nothing is changed in him: the same prayer, the same love! But Jesus must be the example.

Blessed Charles de Foucauld was happy to be poor and destitute of means, because only in this manner could he encounter the Cross—the poverty of Jesus. Love for God and love for neighbor are not only noble deeds of honor or mercy; it is the life, the same life, that, for a Christian, means to be in Communion with God. No matter if this sometimes causes pain, "because upon the wing of pain the soul climbs up again to God" (Michelangelo).

Conclusion

For more than several decades, poetry has followed rules of themes rather than styles. That means poets are free from meter and prosody. Everything is purer: language, concepts, expressions. The words of the poets (Bellusci's, in our case) are often our themes—expressions of human experience, feelings and emotions—except that in *Roman Incense*, these images are exclusive to a Catholic poet.

It is a beautiful collection that will be appreciated by both critics and readers.

Aldo G. Jatosti
International Literary Critics Association
Rome, October 18, 2018

Preface

This poetry project began in France in 1998 and has extended across twenty years and several continents. As a personal journey, the poems are deeply religious and include existential themes reflected in my first poetry book, *Ontology of Blue*. The poems in this second collection were first inspired by the French mystic St. Thérèse of Lisieux. After I met the late Francesca L'Orfano, a visual artist who became a friend, she encouraged me to pursue the publication of my work and also put me in touch with the poet Pier Giorgio Di Cicco. I had the privilege of visiting with Pier Giorgio during my stay in Toronto in February of 2004.

My fascination with language through Literature (B.A. University of Toronto) and Linguistics (M.A., University of Calgary) culminated in Creative Writing (M.F.A., University of Nebraska). My Ph.D. in Philosophy (Dominican University College, Ottawa) served to probe philosophical questions relating to God, especially Divine Love. From poems that were once personal expressions shared only with a few, I began gradually sharing my writing with the public.

The poems in this collection were also written during the intense spiritual experience of pilgrimages. I am very grateful to Milanka Lachman and 206 Tours who made it possible for me to go on these pilgrimages to Europe and the Holy Land.

"Holy Year" and "Graeco-Roman Meditations" and revisions of the entire manuscript were written during my work periods in Rome. I am especially grateful to Fr. Elio Montelone, who supported me in my writing, including the submission to the Cala Petralana poetry competitions. During my visit to Fiuggi outside of Rome with Fr. Elio in 2015, and while staying at the Sisters of St. Elizabeth Guest House, we met Signora Anna Maria Marfè, who put me in touch with her husband Professor Aldo Jatosti. Both were organizers of the Cala Petralana Poetry Prize.

I am also grateful to the community of Brothers at Santa Maria Maggiore in Rome who have shown me warmth and kindness. In this atmosphere of Christian goodness, Dominican fraternity, prayer, and reflection, I was provided with the environment for further revisions to this collection.

I am thankful for my life shared with the Dominican Brothers in Vancouver, British Columbia, who are upholding *Veritas*—and doing so with joy! I am truly grateful for their caring presence.

Rome
August 15, 2018

I thank God for my family:

My sister, Maria, and her husband, Arduino; my brother Michael and his wife, Anna; my nephew David, his wife Veronica, and their daughter, Isabel Rose; Marco; Daniel and his wife Brenda; their children, Mattea and Gianluca, and their baby-to-be-born; my nieces Bernadette and Rosemary; my nephew Anthony and his wife Irene. To my aunts, uncles, and cousins, living and deceased, in Canada and Italy.

Many priests, religious, and communities have been a source of inspiration and prayerful support throughout the years. I give thanks to God for them. In particular, I wish to acknowledge:

Fr. Patrick Bénéteau, Justin Doucette (CC), Fr. Pablo Munoz Iturrieta (IVE), Fr. Joe Leclair, Fr. Louis Madey; Fr. Paul McKeown (OSM), Fr. Francis McKee, Fr. Ruiz Montealegre (Diocese of León, Nicaragua), Br. Nazar Zukaz (Diocese of Lviv, Ukraine), Fr. Tuomas Nyyssölä (Diocese of Finland), Fr. Francois-Dominique David (FI), Luc Poirier (FSSP), Don Urbano Prencipe †, Br. Gavin Rodrigues (OP), Fr. Michael Ruddick, and Fr. Rodolfo Segura-Garrido (OP).

Sr. Yesennia Guzman Calle (IVE), Sr. Tran Hang (CSC), Sr. Monica of the Blessed Sacrament (OCD, Nairobi, Kenya), Sr. Sarah Rudolph, (IBVM), and Sr. Maria Vianneya (SMDM, Krakow, Poland).

Dominican Nuns of Our Lady of Peace, Squamish, BC; Dominican Sisters of St. Cecilia ("Nashville Dominicans"), Port Coquitlam, BC; Monache domenicane dell'Annunziata,

Rome, Italy; Moniales dominicaines, Berthierville/Sherbrooke, QC; Moniales dominicaines, Rweza, Burundi; Monjas Dominicas, Managua, Nicaragua; Sisters of Life, Toronto, ON.

Benedictine Monastic Community, Mission, BC; Dominican Friars, Goa, India; Legion of Mary, Vancouver Comitium; Saint Mary's Parish, Vancouver, BC; Scalabrini Missionaries, Our Lady of Sorrows, Vancouver, BC.

I thank God for the many individuals whom He has put on my pilgrim journey. I am grateful for their presence, encouragement, and prayerful support:

Ann Birch (RCIA, St. Kevin's Parish, Montreal); Anna Maria Bittonti (Piccole Carmelitane in famiglia, Vancouver); Robert Benoit; Gary and Lise Bourgeois; Yvonne Bulger; Aurélie Caldwell; Malvina Cappellaro; Marian Cowenbergh; Anne Coulombe (former Principle, Our Lady of Sorrows School, Vancouver); Thomas and Czeswala Daniels; Fabiano Dellaera; Jacqueline Duclos; Wanda Gawronska (Associazione Pier Giorgio Frassati); Andrew Goring; Don Guy and Cathy Sanderson-Guy; Shirley Hamre; Robert† and Nora Hoskinson; Peter Paul Ifeanyi; Vesna Jankovic; Gordon Johnson and Beryl Côté-Johnson; Christine Jones (President of Catholic Pacific College); Robert and Lindarae Larocca; Eric Lawrence and Linda Seguin-Lawrence; Daniele Lorenzini; Francesca†, Matteo, and Malia L'Orfano; Linda McCallum; Murray MacLeod and Linda Soulière-MacLeod; Paul Moylan† and Sandra Ayoub; Hidge and Marlene† Murdoch; Brett Marshall; Melissa Monette; Brett Morris and Lisa Fooks; Nicholas O'Brien; Connor Ohara;

Jim Ovens†; Marcela and Lara Paniagua; Hannah Pytlak; Janlyn Rathgeber; Charles, Jacynthe, Mikaella, and Raphael Saar; Anne Sheflin; Lorraine Shelstad; Andrzej and Nicole Skulski; Catherine Thomas; Scott Ventureyra; Joe Zambon.

French Novitiate – I*

*Poems from this section were originally written in French

Doctor of Divine Love

Your story in Lisieux embarks
where Romans, Normans, Elenor and St. Joan
left their mark,
but I on a pilgrimage—alone.

My knees pulled, tears rolled—
you captured me in black and white,
candles flickering, your mystical hold,
Oh, Thérèse! Lead me to Jesus my life!

Humanity trapped by Freud, Marx, and Nietzsche
repressive freedoms unfold;
instead, I brought you home:
journey together, you lead me gently.

Embraced by habits faithful to Rome,
the altars your image project,
triduum—Rosary—offering and poem,
at the flowered table again we met.

Green hills, cracking streams, melodies solemn:
bells dance: patroness of the novice.
"Doctor" proclaimed by His Holiness.
Oh, Thérèse! Show me the way to divine love.

Sunday, October 19, 1997

Prayer of a Novice

Blessed Mother of Trigance,
    I love you!

Our Lady of Saint Julien,
    your beauty fills my heart.

Presented in your royal dress,
    you reign more splendid
    than the mother of Solomon.

The mornings you perfume me with dew,
    your cape sprinkles stars,
    the moon, at night.

In silence monks kneel before you,
    Mother and your Child.
    Help me to grow in the Holy Spirit.

Most Holy Virgin of the Annunciation,
    you remained faithful to the Cross…
    with you I desire the same road:
    teach me to say yes without understanding.

Too long, too hot, the summer days;
    winter's frosty nights torment me.
    Thunder, lightening, storms:
    I'm afraid.

Oh Mother of hope, take me by the hand.

Far from my family; far from friends:
> to you I entrust them.

I feel alone, my Mother, my refuge—
> embrace me with your sweet love.

Trigance (Var), France, 1998

Roman Martyrs

Loire castle, green hills, sheep graze
tunic, scapular, *capuce* flutter,
rosary flows.
Infinite encounters
        forgotten chapel.
Dryness of warm winds
choke
noisy flies attack wounds—cuts.
Dialogue of desire,
        offered to Christ crucified…
Bloodshot eyes, disciples follow,
            on their knees, prisoners tied:
            men, women, Nero's feast,
            calf of gold,
            screaming cries.
Desert devours, truth silenced,
                love burns.

Vigils on a Hill

Hill shines of radiant light
        flames process
mysterious encounter.
Blue sketches fuse with earth
    green birch leaves,
    smooth trunks
        create a corridor.
Ancient chapel hidden
    flicker of candles pierce
    bodies stand and kneel
        angelic flutter
    chants
            clear syllables.
Asperges under stars—
    moon-lit sky.
Prayers for a fatigued world
    perfuming myrrh
        brings rest.
White lilies mark a sanctuary path
    incense rises.

Silence of Monks

On his knees offers his body to Jesus
        hours of prayers punctuate the day.
Alone at the marble altar, the world distant,
        young man consecrates his virginity
to Blessed Mary.
Sun of August burns like passion
bees, birds, and butterflies flap their wings,
habit encloses, suffocates, and purifies.
        Silence—a monastic glance
        one accompanies the other,
        hermetic visits
        to seize the One of contemplative Being.
Mountains protect an abandoned home
grass and trees like velvet extension
        …sun disappears,
        sublime captured by clouds.
Dust road refuses change
        frogs, flies, and mosquitoes follow.
Syllables of a melodic litany.
Moon appears, prayers to Blessed Mary.

David Bellusci

November Consecration

Word of concern, perhaps unsettling
my silence,
with his sharing:
baking bread, following squirrels,
God in his heart,
devoted to Jesus and Mary.
Chanting together we receive
the Miraculous Medal, blessed,
      thrice-kissed:
      prior-friend-and-I.
For the Blessed Virgin, candles flicker
*tout proche** we pray on our knees.
Hidden rocks, dry mud, roman bridge,
birds soar—canticles to God.
Crystal waters reflect, we praise
with Francis.
Year follows, I hear his virginal voice
I remember our act of offering
dreams of Assisi and Rue de Bac
thirst to love and enter Paradise.
November rains arrive, falling
leaves and fog—
my friend disappears
clouds remain…a poem.

close by

Toucher (To Touch)

Between sky and land,
            world fades
Eternal watches, endless rest.

Village stones, green hills,
            winds call.

First Being: cause: principle: source.
        Friends:
                chosen by God?

Entering a chapel, rosary in his hand
        he signs me
        holy water—Cross—
        marked.

I Desire

like John Paul II to teach the Truth,

and with bold Hope of Josephine Bakhita,

as Thérèse of Lisieux follows the way of Love—I desire

the intensity of Bridget of Sweden who wore His wounds

submission to God as Thomas More
defying state and prestige

to comfort the poor like Mother
Teresa of Calcutta and passion

of Mexican *Cristeros*.

To run in muddy fields with the purity
of the children of Fatima

as a disciple of Thomas Aquinas to understand Being,

to defend the Roman Church with the
conviction of Catherine of Siena.

I wish to preach with Dominic, and to
die like the saints with courage,

the Faith of St. Peter, and the tirelessness
of St. Paul, and lead

humanity to salvation by the same Grace

moving Augustine of Algeria.

In the spring perfume of rain, maple sun spills

I think of Kateri Tekakwitha, to dance beneath
the rainbow and burst with joy—

ascend mountains with Pier Giorgio
and contemplate Beauty.

Like music of Sunday bells, sing songs of swallows

with Marcel Van and testify:
    Jesus Christ is my Savior!

Word/s

How I wish, my dear saint,
like you to follow
      Jesus,
        my Savior, my King.
Be my teacher, my sweet friend,
lead me further each day
      to Jesus
      Word of my life.

Words, how many do we hear
day after day? I hide myself in the cloister
of my habit.
Petals and thorns lead me to the Cross
a Johannine offering to Jesus and Mary.

My heart and soul lost in God.

Your blessed words repeat at night,
soul cries silence and solitude…

Pierced by Word of love,
hide me, Jesus, in your heart,
        transform me in Truth.

Heights of Montmorin

Lent this year seemed short
meetings with Jesus intensified.
Satan never ceases to take advantage
of limits—forges alliances.
At Montmorin an octave of joy,
healed. Ascent of my soul
to cleansing blues.
Embraced by leaves, caressing branches
immaculate snow purifies me.
I stretch on a carpet of velvet moss,
with the sun I praise
the Lord who shines his splendor
in the silence of virginal dew.
Enchanted by flowers
and butterflies, the forest a prism
of colors: marigolds, violets, bluebells,
winged creatures flutter emeralds,
turquoise, crystal.
Eternal rhythm of a creek before me,
first white flowers of spring descend.
Hidden with Mary, I meditate
Sacred Words, sleep in the arms
of my Creator God.

April 9, 1999, Montmorin, French Alps

His Eyes Close

Mutilated body, torn flesh,
his head drops in the sun's fire,
absorbs the voices of sorrow, grief
and skies.
His eyes close, his eyes open.
Thorns drip blood…down his arms,
holes reveal the nails
blocking a mother's embrace.
His eyes close, his eyes open.
His heart in flames of love pierced
innocent victim, naked.
Fatigue cannot overpower desire.
His eyes close, his eyes open.
Road carved by heavy wood,
mission enveloped in red satin.
His eyes close his eyes open.
One with the cross, sweet blood
purifies the earth: faithful to God
redeeming agony of a last breath.
He closes his eyes.

Good Friday, St. Jodard (Loire), France

Discernment

Train screeches stop, scattered thoughts
persist.
Rome rattles too loud for a monk.
On a sacred mountain
        joy-filled friars desire—
        voices of praise, share
        Christmas cakes.
Nativity of *Gesù Bambino**
                fleshy colors
                create prints
        of that familiar Child
        festivities with the Blessed Virgin.
Chant joy on their knees
tremble in the cold, Compline ends the eve.

Ancient chapel of the Archangel,
        San Michele, Padre Pio, we kiss,
        touch sacred stone
        and the *Addolorata***
        —intercedes for us…
                our beloved Mother.
Pasta we feast on with recorded melodies,
        dedicated family provides panini
before farewell blessings.

Cassino/Frigento/Gargano, Italy, 1998/99
Visits with the Franciscans of the Immaculate

*Infant Jesus
***Our Lady of Sorrow*

Loyola Chapel, Montreal

scent of independence
Sherbrooke street apartment
new life at 19, Notre-Dame-de-Grace

English Gothic—Jesuits—a chapel
classes, prayers to my Savior

> grotto of Mary covered
> in winter snow

> statue in a hallway, religious past

...
twenty years pass,
I return in a habit

in summer months I embrace Aristotle,

and Mary at her shrine—discrete
in floral lawns stands
on psychology rooftops
to pray for me.

Altars shift, students dwindle
Catholic Mass, rewritten Communion service.

> Call to France, useless permission
> another farewell, at Loyola.
> > Snow falls,
> > philosophy continues,
> > temptations cling…

Lovesong*

Pray in a chapel, love God,
eyes thirst, your heart hungers.
Your curly hair shaven, razor #1,
in your sandals I felt your joy.

Melodious voice in Italian,
you spoke of desire and yearning,
in Spanish you sang
innocent smile.

Hero's leap we recognize and imitate,
little steps of a Franciscan heart
daily struggle—hidden and forgotten,
wounds of love ignored.

Similar journeys we walked,
road made rough of cracks and rock.
In southern France one last time we met,
raindrops covered your eyes, nose, and lips.

We share the same pilgrim road:
slip—fall—broken.

I pray we are reunited in burning love,
victorious, sacred Heart of Jesus.

June 7, 2001
*In memory of a novice…

Abandonment

Montreal-Budapest Italian art
Renaissance Rococo Baroque

      my heart captured at the start
      St. Thomas prays before the Virgin.

Two altar boys smile at the altar in white
together they honor God
      Jonathan and David, what friends, I said
      in French they reply, *Like us!*

Urgent messages from home—signals:
      visits to the hospital.
Family vulnerable, pierced by wounds

      reassured by prayer—healing God.

Letter transmitted, Superior's severe blow
Montreal's holy hill, final farewell—

      praying to Saint Joseph.

Four-day train journey west
chain of events signal destiny—
            like tracks.

Montréal, May 22, 2002

June 16, 2002

Adriatic coast descends...dry
rocky hills—small town gem,
*La Madonna delle Grazie**
tucked in San Giovanni Rotondo:
treasures hidden, secrets kept.

Son of Italy, son of St. Francis
consolation, hope to pilgrims brought.
Gargano's silence no longer felt—
news spreads—signs...works...

Belief—devotion—prayer,
life of a boy united with Christ.
Satan rejected, holiness embraced.
Friar's flesh reveals Divine love.

Sacred Heart he probed
in his Capuchin robes, confessional still stands
by humble sinners visited—waiting...
touch of sanctity—peace restored.

On this day Pope John Paul II proclaims:
modern mystic, wounded he suffered
to bring Redeemer's love:
Saint of all people, Padre Pio.

Our Lady of Grace

David Bellusci

# French Novitiate – II

St. Dominic's Ascent

Your blessed mother today we recall,
noble woman, prophetess
Juan de Aza—you in her womb—
dreams of a dog carrying a torch,

across the World.

Descendant of Guzman,
                Castilian blood,
shield you choose:

black and white cross—
        light dispels darkness

Archpriest-godfather-uncle,
        prepares your path:
holy virgin seeking God,
        you defend Truth.

Eight centuries pass,
distant banners of divine love
reach new Atlantic shores,

        Iberian expedition
Gospel penetrates uncharted lands.

Blue skies reflect a quiet river,
puffy white clouds ripple,
rows of green trees hide these banks,

I wonder…wait…for my mission.

Providence greets us
in fragrant prayers and awesome silence,
trumpet sounds in procession:

let us together soar the Eternal ascent.

Berthierville (Québec), August 2, 2003

Thanksgiving=

Autumn skies paint
=infinite azures.

Celestial messengers
=chime melodies
in yellow red pastels.

Pumpkin colors trumpet:
=harvest time.

Caterpillar=
awakes in morning dew.

In silence spiders use=the magic spool.

Southern wind holds hands=
with breezy sun at noon.

Scented air mixes=
=grassy moss and pine.

Crystal stream chants,

narrates life:

cycle=spiral=

Transcendent
Truth.

All Saints

Quiet November 1st,
        city streets sleep
        in morning silence.

Yellow leaves scattered
beneath massive oak trees.

Unnoticed.

Reflective disciples fill a room
study God—share their trials—
                joyful melodies.

Sacred words of life eternal:

        Body offered.
        Blood shed.

        Resurrection.

David Bellusci

Holy Souls

In November's morning mist
lonely trees stand cold and naked:
dead silence.

Drops of light pierce the fog.

> shape of grey tombs emerge:
> heraldic angels, *Stabat Mater,*
> rows of Crosses.

Cleansing change, peaceful wait.

Dates inscribed
unheard cities
unknown surnames
man, woman, in sacred ground.

Invocation, chant resonates,
voices pronounce holy words

> read in communion,

ritual water sprinkled,

> litany begins.

Cimetière Notre-Dame, Montréal

Nuns in White Habits

Cool current speaks with ice

blue water ripples in ceaseless motion

    St. Lawrence branches
    reflect the setting sun.

Like layers of lace
trees neatly gather,
silent flutter in the wind.

        Stretch of white clouds
        decorate the sky
        follow river's flow

never-ending western glow.

Light assembles Sister in prayer
timeless act:

        angelic voices touch

            the Eternal.

Monastère des Dominicaines,
Berthierville (Québec), November 7, 2003

December 24th

Procession of candles assemble
altar boys in white and black
midnight sky, winter darkness
excitement flows in chilling frost.
Midnight Mass, Christmas carols
celebrate childhood dreams:
Saint Nicholas offers a perfect world
love-filled, joyful:
Christ present.

Engine puffs in the parking lot.
Papa and his friend wait in a warm car,
slippery drive home, December snow,
smell of cigarettes, thoughts of presents.

Chandeliers, bright lights, welcome,
aromas of almonds coat the kitchen,
creamy chestnuts over pastries bake,
walnuts and honey on biscuits spooned
traditions touch Mamma's soft fingers.
Familiar scent, invitation.

Streetlights flicker in late night,
snowflakes fall to prepare.

Soft silence spreads
Papa sleeps into dawn.
   …gentle knock, Mamma whispers:

It's Christmas!

University of Toronto, Twenty Years Later

On St. Joseph street walking,
        yesterday's campus grounds:
Victorian Literature in Carr Hall,
Middle High German across Queen's Park
that Gothic complex, Old English.

        Days and nights in Robart's carrels
hidden,
my imaginary love with a Greek goddess
consumed me,
        I waited for elevators,
        her smile, no more.

Nightly return to Shelbourne
        the high-rise still stands,
        submarine sandwiches
        my midnight dinner
                during Lent.

        Candles flicker
        delicious music
        final farewell.

Sitting at Our Lady of Lourdes
        Easter Mass, Mom visited:
lasagna, lamb, and rice cake feast.

Summer in Berlin, Summer in Siena.

David Bellusci

Coffee at Hart House,
        changing rhythms
           —and friends…Peruvian poet.

                    God remains…

Joseph in the Pews

At university—alone—
St. Mike's student—new—

apartment—classes—library—Church
absorbed by literature,
the mediaeval kind,
living in a past, woken by the present

that familiar cafeteria face—subway
—and St. Basil's Mass,
Italian features distinct
kneels in the back pew

friend—perhaps in prayer,
stranger otherwise,
from Carr Hall to Kelley Library,
study carrels at Robarts
his RC childhood

        did not resemble mine

    to Mass he was brought by his mother,
    with four brothers
    on Lenten Fridays,
    Stations of the Cross…
    —and when girls pursued him,

        he withdrew to God.

David Bellusci

I was five—I think—
on that Passion Friday
meditating:
                mystery of God's love.

English Literature students,
we both followed our dreams:
Joseph returned home, his fiancée waiting,

       and I on my endless quest
            to embrace that hidden God.

Berthierville Prayers

monastic grounds

    winter
    snow

capture

        me

I refuse
    to let go;

        prayers
        desires:

    something
        Sacred

remote roads
distant walls

    body consecrated

        ice
        river
        stir

I possess frozen snow heaps

        company
    of Lenten hymns.

David Bellusci

On Being a Monk

prayers at four, morning stillness

      liberates—
      pure heart
      to praise the Divine

Benedictine—Cistercian—Trappist
God's soft voice, hidden in clouds.

Snow blankets monastery grounds:
silence of Mother Mary.
Dawn orienting perfection

      the Cross.

Chants unite voices, eternal communion,
world ignores

      acts

meaningful, known only to God

an outstanding monk
—alone—
discovers true love in the chapel
Christ crucified draws his heart
listens to Truth revealed by God
present transcending, happiness sought

illuminating the monastery
the majestic sun rises
unveiling holy rites

Silent Wait

Behold!

Message disturbs a virgin,
accept what makes no sense:

> *from God.*

Why me…?

*Others in the neighborhood
can conceive, carry,*

> *be a mother.*

In mystery,

> God chooses.
> God waits. *Yes? No?*

> *Yes, Lord.*

Truth adheres to God's world: reality.
Love desires Supreme Good:

> *I carry your Word:*
>> God growing within
>> silence
>> white winter snow falling
>> virgin virginising.

>> Divine alone.

The enemy waits to devour me.

> *Truth strengthens me.*
> *I know God Is Love.*

David Bellusci

Brother Silence

4:30 a.m. kneels
    in payer

        in the dark
            descends

        room full of laundry

        daily cycle starts:
        washers and dryers

stroll in the cafeteria
black coffee

        hour before Mass
        and Lauds

        orange juice and a toast
        other Brothers stumble in

ghastly rains pour
thick clouds immoveable

        waits for a letter
        someone—anyone—perhaps…

returns to his green-painted
room, familiar garments

folds socks—trouser—t-shirts
decades of white tunics and scapulars

pasted on the wall
        postcards of Mary
        country churches

canaries chirp, swing,

        in Silence Brother smiles

Death of Priests

At a rural mission, somewhere
—remote tombstone:
young missionary from Ireland,
Franciscan sent to Zimbabwe
by his order, serving God
fighting spiritual battles
and malaria,
friar in his twenties not far from Harare (Salisbury)
at the Church he served, was buried.
His loved ones he dutifully left,
now belongs to the communion of saints:
into a new family born.

Cottolengo hospital, bed-ridden
in pain his yellow body we bathed him.
And when I asked him, *How do you feel?*
the Jesuit pointed to the Cross and said,
According to His will.
Drinking difficult, eating not possible.
Fellow Jesuit visited
to bring his brother comfort.
Morning arrived for the ritual bath,
but God finally cleansed him.

Committed to the Gospel he preached,
never forgetting his beads for Mary
he proclaimed what he received.
But years of service slowly wore
the Dominican away,
into fragility.
Seemingly forgotten by the
Quiet Revolution
a culture re-constructed,
Québec ignored the heroic saint.
Friars and family remember:
Veritas writes history.

Buckled Shoe

Only her left shoe I notice
        with my right eye as we sit.

Her limp I can hear
            as she enters,

      her dark green trench coat
      same throughout the year
      —except summer.

She takes her seat
in the pew beside me
each day.

      Discretely I greet her: *Bonjour.*
She whispers her reply
with a delicate smile.

After prayers the woman with a limp
makes her exit.

Moved by her presence
              —I'm not sure why.

When the sun shines on the stained glass
in the morning,
and in the evening
when candles are lit,

I look forward to the woman
with the buckled shoe.

I heard the Sister passed away after
I left the novitiate.

St. Joseph: Prayer of a Novice

Blessed Husband of Mary, you
consoled Jesus
instructed, protected Him
with love.

I embrace you patron of Virgins:
comfort me with your presence:

bumpy roads
meandering crests drop into valleys.

Solitude offers me company,
I am treated to loneliness.

My novitiate endless
—a lifetime:
months before I started,
required preparation on a sacred hill.
Withdrawn and separated, years
pass.
Now I count the days.

Chaste spouse of the Holy Virgin:

teach me to love

       —offering myself.

I seek my beloved Lord:
    His love: as recompense?

    He only asks for my heart.

        That we may be One.

Guide me, Saint Joseph:
    to perfect love

so I may be one with Jesus

        True Love.

Oratory of Saint Joseph, Montréal, 2004

Sea Salt and Oil Lamps

Cassiar Street*

Mamma's voice pierces the morning.

Goosebumps tickle my skin,
too cold to uncover the blankets
rain patters, its unwanted presence.

My name always last, now she's mad.

No time to wash.
No time to brush.
No time to eat.

Uniform loosely hangs,
        blue shirt sticks out,

Sis wears her plaid skirt,
covers her knees, blouse tucked.

Hooting, motions us: "Get in!"
the language Mamma knows best.

She hears our buckles snap,
        her 1970 Malibu glides away.

Wipers swish like a blender
mixing on low.

Silent in the back seat, Mary's
head against the window, I know.

Trees vanish in the steel and cement.

Now the intersection—

>Cassiar Street:
>foot on the break.

Now Mamma checks:

>Left.
>>Right.
>
>Left.

Now Mamma takes charge:
>they wait for her.

Mamma pushes my head back.
Mamma moves forward.
>Stopping:
>Trucks: Trailers: Buses:
>Pick-ups: 4-wheel drives.

So we could get to school on time.

*First published in *Writing Cultural Difference* (Toronto: Guernica, 2015)

Papa's Chair*

An oak back, strips
hold frame comfortable, but hard.
Worn colors, chocolate
brown to toffee, shades,
smooth sides, round corners
clovers carved into shape.

The chair stands on four legs,
as if waiting, since the forties.

Paper by the desk,
sheets crisp, ready, whispering
"Have a seat, write."
      siedete, e scrive nu poc.'

For scribbling, a blue pen to the right,
photographs of family
deliberately positioned.

La Madonna, pink, blue,
red plastic flowers.

Magazines from Padova,
local Italian papers piled
on night table, beside chair.
Opened envelopes folded triple
elastic bands, Italian stamps,
huge dictionary bought in Milan,
discoloured, falling apart.

Saints watch from four walls,
Padre Pio speaks each month.

Papa pensively mutters,

the unfinished letter, to his sister,
the one person in Italy
he remained close to. Expressing
thoughts in ink, over days, completed.

Now, a letter to his best friend, Don Michele.

Another, to one of the Italian
orphanages. A letter to the Mother
Superior, to thank her
for the photo of the orphans.

Papa refused the new chair that
Mamma bought.

But he agreed to the desk.

*First published in *Writing Cultural Difference* (Toronto: Guernica, 2015)

Sister Mary

Her mother curls her hair
                gold locks that fall
with her Communion veil

                white lily in her hand.

God's path leads to charitable Sisters
on another coast…

           daily prayers—teacher?
                        Communion with God.

High school years she divides:
        books chapel Mamma
                      home
                      work

holy convent her heart remains fixed.

        God's plan…

        husband—children to fill her heart
            Sunday after Sunday
            holds her little five
                family Mass,
      suits—dresses—Italian socks

            silence learned:

        helps Mamma baking lasagna
        provides Papa company with coffee
        sends packages to
Zimbabwe—Ivory Coast—Ethiopia

    Evening ends
        in solemn thanksgiving.

Angel Voices

I hold the cold phone,

    past...   *presence* of desire:

his voice deep—mature

    child's smile cheers me

energetic greeting follows

    little lady—her ribboned hats imagined

to answer his series of questions

    I remember holding his hand
    walk down a busy street

        I miss

high-pitched melody—excited

    her care-free laughter
    engaging me with blue eyes

        named after a saint

brown curly hair in my thoughts,

    gentle voice, chosen words
    artwork of a boy grown up.

Picture of a Shepherd Boy

In a parish hall he stands on stage
eyes focused
his words pierce
—childhood
excitement of Christmas plays.
Winter days blanketed in snow,
green-red-blue lights in dark streets.

Each syllable clear,
consonants and vowels
shape his lips.

Manger scene: paper rocks create a stable,
boy and girl and Baby Jesus.

His child's body articulates
God's promise.
Robed in light blue, rope ties his waste,
white-head cover, he gathers sheep
drawn by a star pointing to Jesus.

Chairs transport me,
                to a starry sky…

My Nephew's Canvas

fingers delicate
      smooth skin of an artist

grey: blacks—green: blues:
      canvas experiment

forceful mountains overlook calm lakes
      Nordic scenes, evergreens

imagination guided, senses feel
      emotions painted

meditating the theme
      object and subject unite

the transcendent imposes itself
      on the paint

artist and creation divide
      an interior story expressed

reach out—above—beyond
      a prayer to the silent God

waits for colors to answer
      hidden form, new meaning

deep eyes seek a message of truth
      contemplation brushed.

Emily in Carmel

She sits comfortably
in a cafeteria chair
legs folded,
devoted student of Computer Science.
Stares at her coffee, pensive expression
accompanies her elegant
jacket and skirt—
delightful smile.

She wears a broach,
completes the details of her life.

Me a nun? She chuckles loud,
question absurd,
too polite to reply.
Her coffee cup in a firm grip.

University students, we study until dawn
she in her labs, I in my office.

Weekends invite reflection:
God and *chai*, more *chai*, and still God.

Chirps begin, pink light follows
walks across the residence lawns
after-degree-dreams.

Career—fashion—family
she offered them all:

    my true friend preferred
    God and Carmel.

David Bellusci

Consecrated Virgin

She joined us in prayer:
>dark wavy hair
>casually dressed
>baby-face full of joy and life
>perfect mother and wife.

Faithful to our group,
she attached herself
>sharing her stories
>and testimonies
>speaks to high school students
>on that forgotten subject:

>>virginity.

In love with God and Truth
>her dream she shared
>naïve fragrance
>of innocence.

Her prayer:
>to be a mother of many,
>big family she desired
>and a good man who shared her dream:
>wifehood and motherhood.

Rosary prayers continued,
one week after the next,
and my blessed friend continued

    on her determined path.

A letter I received
months after my departure
telling me how much she loved God.

Her dream was fulfilled
a mother she became,
of numerous children
more than she expected.

    God generously answered
    in His own way:
    my friend, consecrated Virgin.

Rue Saint-Sulpice

Decorated trees of ice crystals
       layered lace line tree tops
       cool particles

Neo-Gothic basilica directs
       noble pieces of tiles columns statues:
       contrasts carved—brushed
       pathos—sacrifice.

       Musica sacra fills the temple
Platonic forms realized
Triumph of Beautiful:

       Mary *handmaiden* of God.

White snowflakes coat
       winter branches
       falling into *dolcissimo:*
       blue lights dress the season.

Notre Dame royal
transcends French religion

       Rue des Sulpiciens.

       Parisian lamp-posts light
       narrow cobble stone streets

       fur coat spectators stroll
       whistling melodies…

Saint Michael's Cafeteria

Centered blue painting—Archangel—
white feathers spread
wings flutter
spear in hand.

Students engage in cafeteria chatter
iPods and embraces—
Latinos—Asians—Slavs—Celts—Blacks.
[Chaucer and Shakespeare my lunch time
break.]

…

Now a conference paper, I return.
Curry salmon. No dessert. Friday evening.
Thoughts of eating chocolates
during Lent filled with guilt.
Sin? Vice? Or both?

Plato's *Symposium*, Aristotle's
Nicomachean Ethics,
St. Augustine's
Confessions: Love and Truth.

Question asked at fifteen—
What is happiness? And still…

David Bellusci

Office Hours

Mr. McNaught's slender body
blocks his bay window
soft sounds of summer rain drench
his hidden thoughts—poked
by my Chaucer text, a question
on Bath's wife.

I upset his melancholic reflection
questions about tempting iambs
and seducing meters. McNaught's
nose follows my index finger:
Chaucer's pilgrims probed.

Re-buried under books, I find my
path to tapes—my morning ritual:
Prologue: Listen: Speak: Repeat.
Canterbury pilgrims chanting
Middle English rise—fall—I
hold my pilgrim cane.

Wet branches tickle my skin. Cool
April rain mystifies our muddy
path. Pines like medicinal herbs
offer potion-like cleansing. We
clap and cheer the sacred sight
of Canterbury, St. Thomas à Becket
remains…

A timely gaze out my window,
marble statue of Mary, I invite
my students to reflect:
not Chaucer…but Thomas More.

Teachings of a Mystic

Listen to the ocean waves

massive smashes soothe, heal,

endless caresses, a mantra—

wash:

stress, high anxiety,
repression, dissociation,
neither Freud nor Jung can treat.

Ocean purifies, eternal
rhythm calms, rests, finds its
source in the Divine,
First Cause.

Hume fundamentally erred
skeptical philosopher
no illuminating faith
sophistically reasoned
the irrational.

Hildegard von Bingen
Benedictine mystic, understands
nature's powers.

Her instructions surpass Design.

God is the source of all that is

True and Good.

Sacred Space

Looking down, they gently shut
my office door,
not just because they probe thoughts
on Plato and Aristotle:
—they question themselves—
perhaps a confession.
Words, pure and simple resonate
love of God,
bodies ache, holiness sought,
battles. God's grace pierces them,
cleansed of evil gripping.
I point to Ephesians six: real war.
Virgin bodies revirginized, minds victory
in abstinence. Oak and bronze crucifix
comfort. Italian fresco of Mary
reassures. I ask them to profess prudence,
use force, absolutes for holiness,
non-negotiable, God's divine power.
Pure mind means:
vision of God.
I agonize with them re-molding
warped human nature:
true being reached in chastity.
When the semester closes, I may hope
to recognise their footsteps.
Faces—stories—crosses,
accompany me at each Mass.

Tombstones

Cold grey stones stand alone, silent wait
engraved names claim each tomb
chipped angel wings unveil their age.

Saints tell stories of the dead—RIP:
for the visitor and the mourner.

Margaret born in 1915, *a good wife.*

And a baby died after a few months,
taken up by the Divine Creator.

Neighbors knew about James
hanging from the tree, choked to death.
Wife left him and took the kids.
The good priest offered him a decent burial.

In the cloudy month of November,
the Romans remember their dead.

…

He wears his hockey sweats,
as if lost, reading names—stops:

                                      kneels.

Widow in the Pew

Senhora sits alone in the front pew
always at the very end
never misses Mass.
She attends in heavy
snowfall in her plastic boots
in scorching summer heat
windy rainy days under a bent
umbrella.
I recognise her cough when she enters
Smiles—teeth missing—
barely grasp her words.
If I knew the nouns—verbs—
adjectives to inquire...
Senhora prays
in her language,
knows God understands everyone.
If *senhora* misses Mass
(happens only on weekdays)
I know she is bed-ridden.
I wonder how *senhora* lives
with no husband; I never see her children,
or maybe she has none.
An envelope *senhora* offers me
whispers, *Missa,* memorial offering
her husband's soul.
And when I read the name
senhora's eyes fix at the altar.
In her wrinkly hand she holds
a black Rosary, approaches
for Communion, so the Holy Eucharist

David Bellusci

blesses the cold palm. A pious tradition.
Whenever we have
a collection she finds money
for the basket—
even St. Anthony's poor box does not
go unnoticed.
I always wanted a picture
with her, the two of us:
black veil
black dress
black shoes
black rosary

                    and halo.

Caribbean Outpost

Citadel guards the island

threats:

blasting seas crush the hill

observing observers observed. Pathway
to Imperial Virgin Islands

hidden gems.

Baptizer opens the way, Gospel:
flag—church—language:

        whose   Flag?
        whose   Language?
        whose   Church?

Cathedral celebrates five hundred years:
national identity—religious historical.

Island claimed: *Spanish—Roman Catholic*

                      English—French—Dutch

city not far waves orange
        colonial mistress airport's name—
        —imposed earthly monarch.
        Laws created at distance—
        lectures on rights and freedoms
        Western paradoxes.

Fortress withstands attacks—at first.
Baptizer stands opposite,
                bulldozer.

San Juan de Puerto Rico, 2013

Plaza Bolivar

Dark columns—regal,
yellow-blue-red stripes
support
wave
peach-stone plaza contrasts
bluish sky

Quote from Santander:

> *Arms gave you Independence,*
> *Laws will give you freedom.*

Cathedral overlooks the square—
baroque of Santafé,
sacred Spanish.
Two towers. Virgin centered.

Faithful enter. Faithful exit—
oak doors into eternity.

> *Religious Santafé will prosper.*

Mary clothed
black in mourning,
brown of Mount Carmel.

Boy appears with the priest
flows in his black soutane.

Voice calls me to repentance.

Bogotá, Colombia

Sopa de Queso (Cheese Soup)

Lent in Nicaragua means
abstinence—some effort
to observe penitential journey:
                desert.
Lunch at a Nica restaurant
Friday with family, time for friends
food smells of delicious *queso*,
"Cheese soup." Trays of bowls,
table to table, Nicaraguan dresses.
                But, cultures abandon
religious practices
replace exterior with interior
but nobody notices
and everyone forgets. Exterior
acts signal:
                prayer, abstinence, fast.
Nicaraguans remember.
Shops sell *queso* soups
made from dry cheese, milk, cream,
flour, chile, and menthe.
Catholic culture—pious disciples
until pseudo-spiritual super seculars
convert to inevitable apathy.

Monsoon Prayers

Darkness disappears
                in silence.

Young men in white habits shuffle,
rhythm of Rosary beads.
            Two red lamps centered:
            Crucifix.

Saint Dominic stands, his dog holds
the torch, flame of Preachers.

Immaculate Mary to the right
palms open announce Truth.

Rooster crows repeat, buried
by hiss of palm leaves,
whipping monsoons.

Light unveils the curve of coconut
trees. Bird songs and cricket clatter
pour into the chapel.

            Superior's knock:
            prayers commence.

Scapulars and tunics graciously fold,
voices chant
with sparrow and shrikes.

David Bellusci

Shiny black hair over white *capuces*,
consecrate pews, bow thrice forward.

Monsoons return.
                                        Light burns.

Dominican studentate chapel
Goa, India

Goan Intersections

Three women in bright saris
rhythmically cross the road like
elegant swans, wrapped in peach and orange,
pink, crimson, and saffron.
Little boy holds
his mother's hand.
Scooters pass on both sides
around potholes or cracks
filled with rain.
Adolescent boys, Indian
and Portuguese
wear Rosaries hanging:
one holds by the waist, another the bars.
Palace-like home, this one grape,
three stories and scaffolding,
hide dusty shacks, sheets of asbestos,
nailed boards, dogs guard.
White crosses mark corners,
candles lit in Marian shrines,
Santa Cruz chapel, white
and blue. Christ the King commemorated
three hundred years, memorial
in Portuguese. Hindi signs opposite.
Truck is trapped, blocks angry drivers,
small cars slip through.
Curry samosas fry, *take-away*.
Boar chomps on thick grass,
smoke hides burning garbage,
not the smell.
Moist leaves scattered announce
monsoons.

Nagpur Candles

Descent in monsoons, thick clouds
        coat Nagpur.
Cheerful face
welcomes me in congestion of circulating
traffic. Driver once guided me through Goa,
we later met in Rome, now he leads me—
                India's center.
Ascent to emerald green grounds,
        "Seminary Hill"
where Irish planted a white-and-black cross.
Diocesan seminarians, institutes,
St. Francis de Sales their patron—a Salesian connection?
Cathedral school and college,
        Nobertines, Pallottines, Dominicans,
            fields filled with screams of muddy soccer…
He prepares the bamboo room, a chapel,
to receive the Word:
            candles lit
            his pillow placed opposite
            where I take my place,
            he is
            in white, attentive, listens,
            his *guru,* or *rabbai,* or *priest.*
            I call him *brother.*
                Namaste.

Dominican Ashram, Nagpur, India

Paris Kneels

La Seine lights her reflection
décembre, fêtes de Noel:

soirée café, student clubs, weekend
party-goers. *Ville de joie,**
screaming bands,
they inhale St. Denis.
Chardonnay, Kronenbourg
*pression,** soak in buzz…

!!! Red flashes. !!! Red swords.

*Joie** silenced. City mourns.
+ Cross targeted + once more +

Crumbling empire forgotten
revelers crawl soaked in blood.

Wet in tears—she turns—to God

promises fidelity to her boyfriend…

                     fireman killed.

city of joy
**draft beer*

David Bellusci

Turtle and Elephant

In front of a bookshop, pilgrim flags,
clerics in black, veiled women hold
their jingling cup.
Eyes opposite he questions me,
secretly reveals a bracelet, slid
smoothly onto my wrist.
René from Cape Verde, colonized
by the Portuguese. Lusophone
Africa -- I only visited Mozambique.
St. Peter's
to my left, René returns, now greets
me with an elephant, then a turtle.
Asking what they have in common:
*the elephant is slow, the tortoise is slow,
and they both live a long life. May you
live a long life,* he said, *and pray for
my baby, that he may be strong.*
The turtle raises its head, the elephant
trunk curled back, glossy burned red,
coats shell and skin. I remember René
the Capoverdian and his baby,
that they may find Eternal Life.

Hills of Umbria

Medieval stone walls, stand
collapsing
    into green pastures, whisper,

lead
    sheep and shepherds
    home.

Tall grass sings of God, sacred

Angelus bell tolls:

    Land of hermits—mendicants—saints
        ascent of eastern mystics
        Umbrian mountain caves
        Roman Christendom

    birth place of western monks.

Il Poverello hid in the mountain wounds

    of the Saviour

transforms his world—our obsessions.

Cloistered nuns—disciples—foundresses

women of iron
scent of pure soap

lilac.

In silence animals graze
distant bells ring

in the Hills of Umbria.

"Vision of St. Dominic"

She holds the Christ Child
he kneels before Mary
fingers on the Rosary.
St. Dominic kisses the beads
on his palm, three fingers upward,
his index and thumb touch.
His kiss is gentle.
Capuce and scapular,
candle-light layers covered
in a black cape,
white folds in prayer.
St. Catherine in ecstasy
crowned with thorns
of glory,
right hand presses against her heart,
Divine union.
Child turns to His Mother, assured.
Pure flesh,
lamb to be slaughtered.

Mother presents her Divine Son.

(Bernardo Cavallino, 1616-1656)
National Art Gallery, Ottawa

My Tower

Morning sunlight peeks
        through my window

I wake up to my father's crucifix
    once
    on his coffin,

and my mother's funeral photo
    kept
    on a bookshelf.

From the southwest tower

facing Saint Anthony's
    Servites of Mary
    celebrate Mass in Italian.

Looking
southwest
    along the river
    Capuchins at Saint Francis
    offer Sacraments in French.

Autumn leaves fall
from the East.

        Branches

        disappear

into the dead
of winter.

My tower is empty—

>   except for God…

Facing East

In a uniform row
their complexions rosy
blonde hair some reddish
black frizzy hair or straight
they stand to attention alert
responding to their navy
berretta leader.

I turn around to face
the huge rock and morning sun
I wait for their queue
Latin hymn.

Red autumn leaves fall
in the cool wind.
Evergreen firs gently sway
offer a scent of pine.

A Greek altar cloth placed
on the stone,
candles blown out, relit.
He holds the flag
of the Sacred Heart,
motionless.

Each approaches me
my hand and fingers
slightly raised.
In silence still
Divine union
they kneel
one by
one.

Indie Music

My nephew explained the genre:
mixed, sentimental, past.

Summer ends, trees shake green,
mid-September closes,
autumn orange, opens.
Stars on East Hastings at 5:30 a.m.
Sunday morning coffee.
No traffic.

Dressers I emptied
of music cassettes:
Breton troubadours, Indian masala,
Persian candles, Italian gelati.
Deleted. Disposed.
Bomboniere* from Baptisms, First Communions,
car, Rosary, candy dish.
Wedding confetti.

File cabinet, African research, field work,
South Africa hiking to Ivory Coast,
Ethiopian Airlines to Nairobi, train (Dar es Salaam)
bus (Lusaka) to Harare.

God's will?

Missionary, I thought.

Mamma offered me her smile,
last farewell.
Papa gave me his blessing,
from a hospital bed.

Rome again, not my plan.

favors

Roman Sun

Clear morning bells ring seven
times sunlight spills in the terrace
August trees—green, soft blue sky.
*Giardino degli Aranci.**

Piazza Venezia imposes
black angels and chariots
Tiber pushes its way
winding in Rome.
Copula on Vatican hill, dominates

Italian Renaissance,
piazzas and fountains.
Rebirth, new life in the sacred city.

Stones shaped and worn, unveil
ancient story:

Caesar's or Peter's flags.

Bicolour—
orange: red—Imperial Rome.
yellow: white—Christian Rome.

Tricolour—
green: white: red—King's peninsula, Sacred capital
contested unity.

Martyrs and saints, nuns and bishops,
carved Roman roads.

Garden of Oranges (park in Rome)

Graeco-Roman Meditations

Interior Fortress

Marcus Aurelius,
pensive writings in Greek
directs Roman armies,
                Stoic searches,
marble column stands in the irony
      of his memory.
               Worldly glories
                  Aurelius despised.
Death and decay
inevitable.
                Forgotten.
Family, books, tutors failed.
Roman prefect commands Justin's
execution and his students—
seekers of truth.
The Aurelian *colonna*
        removed Marcus and wife.

The true Word stands proclaimed
by St. Paul.
Logos enlightens and saves.

Piazza Navona: Northern Fountain – Late October

Neptune aims his battle
trident,
I'm expected to witness.
Spear.
Aegean
blows thick hair.
Cupids
spit.
Ocean god's eyes intense,
right thigh moves forward,
rock secure:
strikes.
Octopus tentacles
suck Neptune's muscular legs.
Smooth cut through the head.
Sea-horses and mermaids
jubilate
spraying nymphs.
Cupid's circle
spins.

Ice cream drips.

Piazza Navona: Center Fountain – Late November

Caracalla's Obelisk lifts high
the Cross,
unites four gushing rivers,
gods govern each.
Lion emerges—hidden—in splashes
intruders warned. Silent attack.
Ganges holds an oar, navigates
sacred Indian shores.
Nile seeks African source, Ethiopia?
Rio de Plata raises his hands, torn
between snake and silver.
Danube extends loyal hands
to Innocent's dove and twig.
Bernini's baroque meditation:
Pamphili's ecstasy,
Anno. Cal. MDCLI.
Romans complained, moved their
market, floods produced feasts.
Damatian's stadium for *agones*,*
from Tevere to Trevi,
Roman rebirths in rivers.

Blankets wrap white-wine drinkers.

competitions

Piazza Navona: Southern Fountain – Late December

Four tritons blow
from double-flutes. Scaly
legs as if kneeling,
tails wrap.
Bearded faces, thin—thick,
cheeks puff.
Eight masks, expressions
unmoved: still.
Moor stands naked
on a shell
tousled hair—oceanic force.
Thighs bulge, tightened ribs,
dolphin caught,
tail in hand.

Merry-go-round horses dance.

David Bellusci

Voyage of the Soul

White crystals brighten.
Fallen pearls
      lighten my steps.
        Icy waters flow and crack
in silver drops.
              Sun unveils springtime—
                cherries.
I mount a horse
        into massive clouds we fly
        blue and purple skies—
    Venus glances
        flickering lights point to the passage.
Majestic dance of velvet seduces
      infinite silence:
      Eternal.
      Signals the End
of the journey.
Mounted midnight
to contemplate
      the Sacred.

Narcissus

You penetrate the water
hands hold you up
head still.
Sleeves rolled to your elbows.
Eyes fixed.
Straight nose, neck, forehead reflected.
Lips open.
Your eyes almost closed
delight—wonder—desire—invite.
You.
I hear you breathe.
You push yourself gently forward,
shoulders direct your kiss: mirror.
Moved. Unmoved.
Your image
unmatched complexion contours
you contemplate.
Head spins
flesh, symmetry
into eternity, as if,
Immortal.

Galleria Nazione di Arte Antica, Rome
(Michelangelo Caravaggio, 1571-1610)

Piazza del Pasquino

Vittorio Emanuele breathes west.
Piazza Pantaleo
leads to Pasquino's statue—
you third century Hellenist!
Parione's nostalgia,
companion to Domiziano's stadium,
Navona's Baroque—or Innocent's Dream.
Via del Governo Vecchio,
Cardinal Carafa's neopolitan
artist's eye—corners.
Pasquino stands:
> *you talk too much!*
> politicians, patricians,
> *pasquinate* attached.*
> > bold critics.
> *Pasquino, you, listen!*
Adrian, Sixtus, Clement failed
to drown you—silence for ever.

> Pamphili's presence surpasses.

*political/personal notes

Fuoco Rubato (Stolen Fire)

In darkness I stand
        centered on a bridge
water splashes below
hypnotically
        against a brick wall of my life.
Unexpected light surprises—full moon:
Circular disk—
        shield blocks the heavens
stars hidden by a torch
lighting the sky.
        Prometheus is dressed for battle,
            steals fire. Zeus's anger lances
flashes of lightening.
            Bolts roar.
    Ambrosia disappears, the work
of Tantalus.
        Rain pours, I smell the nectar
mixed with fennel.
        My clothes soaked, the scent of divine breath
intoxicates me.
        Head spins from the fermented juices,
I shiver…
White horse spreads its wings—he lands.
        I mount the Pegasus,
        ascend towards the rising sun.
        My name is called…

Submitted to XXII "Cala Petralana"
Olbia (Sardegna), 2017

Gallerie Alberto Sordi (Colonna)

Via del Corso and Largo Chigi—Triton's road
column for Aurelius.
Marble pillars, Vittoriano designs
granite bannisters shield windows,
stained glass roofing, green and gold,
diamond squares, tiled floors,
brass lamps between shops:
      Art Nouveau
      Made in Italy.
Basilica beyond the doors,
*Deo in hon. Mariae Virginis Matris,**
Santa Maria in Via.
Evening espresso, *cioccolato fondente,***
end of November,
Roman chill.
He brings his baby in a stroller:
black coat and blue hat, loose cotton scarf,
grey sweater, wide buttons.
She window-shops: skin-tight pants,
knee-length grey coat,
long brown hair.
Tourists stroll, *Rome, Milan, Venice*
shopping bags.
I drink the chocolate in teaspoons.

    To the Glory of God in Honor of the Blessed Virgin Mary
                                    **hot chocolate milk*

Slaughter of the Innocents

Embraces her baby, shields him
from the merciless soldier, his bulging veins,
arm hard, muscles tight, ready to stab.

Boy in her arms, she moves swiftly,
baby's hand struggles for freedom,
as if knowing his fate.

Hides her boy wrapped in a blue dress,
he submits to paranoid orders, struggles
to rip an innocent child.

Woman lies trying to rescue her infant
from his sword,
central figure, baby pulled by his left leg.

She kneels over her baby, arms protecting
her little one. To kill the infant means
to kill her.

Baby boy pulled by his arms, hanging
like a lamb, mother tugs at the soldier
ready to strike him dead.

Woman's fleshy back uncovered,
vulnerable, breast-feeding,
little one in deadly silence.

Galleria Nazionale d'Arte Antica, Rome
(Jacoppo Negretti, Venezia, 1548-1628)

Parmigianino – Barocci*

Your gaze—a metaphor:
focus on me—head turns slightly
black velvet hat, smooth nose, lips
thin, red. Parmigianino's eyes:
come this way…
Dark beard, black eyes, Barocci
points to the *Flight into Egypt*.
Jesus takes cherries
from Joseph,
guardian father, joyful Babe
rosy-cheek resemblance.
Carpenter's arms concealed,
chosen father He trusts.
Mother-centered—red and blue,
braided hair, over crystal water
hands outstretched.

Exhibition (Musei Capitolini), Rome

Holy Year

Silent Words on Sacred Cloth

On the left-side of the image,
a face sketched, marked
dark red. Helmet of thorns
shapes the head. Inverted 3 on
the negative, 3 on the positive—
the forehead.
Further left, hands joined,
reddish spot, marks deepen
upwards from hands to shoulder.
At the center, man's left side
deep-red triangular shape.
Very end his feet visible,
dark opening covers one foot.
Right-side of the image,
series of incisions,
across the back…cut legs.
Every sign of a man tortured.
Instruments of pain.
Judgment and punishment
—criminal,
unless the accusations—false.
Is love a crime?
He was betrayed because of greed.
Or lust. Or envy.
Were his wounds caused
by rejection? Or abandonment?
His greatest pain—
sins—of humanity that pervert,
distort.
At the end he stood alone.

Solitude.
His most intense human experience
of that "cup"
which he knew and accepted
—alone.
The wounds of Our Lord are for my sins,
my brokenness. There is no greater love
than the love of Jesus.
He has graced me with His love—
He has called me to love others, with

His love—
He has called me to obedience, as He is.
To be poor and chaste, as He is.
To forgive, as He forgives, even
those who betray us, slander us,
misjudge us, abandon us.
The wounds of Our Lord are wounds
that forgive
because to love is to forgive,
and to be obedient
is to be united with God's love.

Before the Holy Shroud, Turin
Friday, June 19, 2015

Prayer Before Salus Populi Romani*

The flicker of ten candles, I process,
before you I kneel, *Deo gratias*. To honor
you, *Regina Coeli*, on this Saturday
morning of August. Holy Year approaches,
I re-consecrate myself to you
—Czestochowa and Altötting, now at Mass.
A blessed day when Pope Pius XII proclaimed
your privileged title. Graces you obtain
for me. An abundance. What should I do?
Graces to be shared.
I want to be Pure:
help me grow in Purity,
that I may discern with a pure heart,
and bring others to Purity, for the Pure
will see the Face of God. That women
and men listen to me with a pure heart.
I desire Courage to proclaim and defend
the truths the Catholic Church teaches,
from Scriptures, Tradition,
the Supreme Law of God, Natural Law.
That criticism, persecution, slander
will not weaken me, but fortify me.
Let humility be my guide, to rid me
of pride, Satan's cunning, twisted
reasoning. Let Humility manifest
how dependent I am on Divine Grace,
that keeps my heart beating.

By your intercession, O Holy Mother
and by the Grace of God, that I may lead
lost souls to your Divine Son,
Jesus Christ, Our Lord and Savior.

Amen.

Santa Maria Maggiore, August 22, 2015, Rome

*Chapel of the Madonna

Visitors at the Basilica

Seven a.m. weakened darkness lifts piazza traffic
pilgrim buses backed since half-past six. Gates unlocked.
Italian military positioned.
Hymns from the Madonna chapel sung.
Seminarians with black backpacks,
glide in one direction.
Sisters in white habits, process along
confessional walls. A student in jeans kneels
for Confession before morning Mass.
Footsteps in the majestic Basilica dedicated
to the Mother of God.
Silence.
Front oak doors open and shut, blowing a cool wind.
Bells ring.
Red confessional lights visible, prayers of *Misericordiae*.
Alleluia chanted.
Eight chimes, followed by a softer one. Corinthian columns
stand beneath Marian mosaics, Sicilian or Syrian?
Hard marble cold, heated by warm hands joined.
Sanctus repeated.
Tourists trickle in, click of camera,
Make room for selfie-sticks. Voices mumble
Latin inscriptions.
Agnus Dei resonates with coughs and footsteps,
unzipping jackets. Line-up at confessionals.
A couple receive a priestly blessing.

Hum of tourists interrupted: cross bearer and thurible, opening hymn, Canons and Bishops proceed, incense rises. Altar of God ascended. Father holds his little girl, mother rocks her baby in a lullaby. Cardinal makes the Sign of the Cross.

Third Week of September

Rome scatters clouds,
melancholy reminiscence
of Marcus Aurelius,
dirge of lamentations.
Lights disappear
yield to *mattino** cobblestones.
Vespas.**
Sisters flutter, veiled in white habits,
Roman-collar priests
glide on Via Merulana.
Unlit shops, beggars in coats
shiver under hats and blankets.

Like a hand covering an oil lamp,
autumnal equinox—half-past seven.

Basilica echoes empty voices.

*morning
**Italian scooters

San Martino ai Monti

Sun spills on the cobble road
filling Piazza
San Martino ai Monti.
      Brick Capocci Tower fitted with secretive
windows of seven floors.
Undefeated mediaeval power—Arcioni family—
replaced by Viterbesi* wealth,
facing Graziani's construction
Daughters of Mary dwelling attached
to a *torre*—admission
        to Esquilino. Dominican nuns secluded,
        hearts
        fixed on Christ, company of Augustinian prayers,
next door separated by solid walls of silence.
Carmelite Curia introduced
          by Mary's cement scapular.
Third-century basilica,
San Silvestro and San Martino,
call to community—even in hiding.

*inhabitants of Viterbo

Sacristy Prayers

Cool wind, dawn showers
my black cape
               wet,
Suor Caterina removes
               the bolt.
Buongiorno,
      sister disappears
like mist in a valley.
             Darkness fills
the morning space
bars protect the windows.
               Rain patters.
               Silence unchanged.
Sacristy lights flicker,
candles and lanterns
replaced.
         Crucifix hangs
         picture of Baby Jesus
         calendar of Lourdes
             Saint Dominic.
                 Ordo.
Alb—Stole—Chasuble—
             Prayers.
Silence.
         Nearby bell chimes.
         I bless myself.
The grilles separate us.
         I kneel…
               Altar of God.

Sante Domenicane (Dominican Saints)

Appear in their white habits:

>one holds a lamb,
>St. Agnes of Montepulciano

>stigmatised, she holds the Crucifix,
>St. Catherine Ricci

>*Dialogues* at her side,
>St. Catherine of Siena.

The three saints walk in my direction.

>>Nuns wait in prayer.

>Vision from the grille.

After Mass one nun surprises me
>has one hand on the grille
>the other holds a letter she reads
>>written for her profession
>>over forty years ago:

Her love for our founder
and for the priests.

Words of fidelity, her voice quivers—

>>she wanted me to know…

>>Fidelity perfected by grace.

Joy of the Cloister

My sister greets me at the bolted door
cool Roman morning, she smiles
in her cheerful voice—invites me
to the sacristy, alb—chasuble set.
Sister flutters away in her habit.
Sanctuary separated
by monastic grille. Five nuns
listen, sing, and pray.
Oak choir for fifty, a statue of Mary.
Before me St. Pius V—painting
       with four nuns, entrusted *monache*
       domenicane dell'Annunziata*—
       Trajan's Tower—*via Alessandrina* or Tor de' Conti,
         first convent, Annunciation mural remains.
I offer the sacrifice at the Altar of God.
Each Sister arrives for Communion, holds
her paten, slightly behind the grilles.
Joy of their hearts illuminates their eyes…
I step outdoors, sunlight
fills the brick streets
Monte S. Martino,
my heart cries out with joy, having drunk
from this Roman fountain.

                        **Dominican nuns of the Annunciation*

Reliquaries of Conjugal Love

Red altar candles flicker, centered
on a black and white photo,
    wife: husband,
earthly ties, Christ's Love sanctifies.
Priest and Scriptures reveal
God's will, conjugal embrace.
    Union consummated:
    sacred bed shared
    ordained by nature,
blessed by God's mediator.
Daughters you bore, instructed
in Truth—eternal Life.
    A mother dies in hope.
Silent footsteps empty your
Normandy home. Carmel
stripped you, jacket and dress.
    Daughters sacrificed:
behind a locked grille, joyful veil.
    A father's tears wiped.
Your relics in Rome, prayers:
Saints Zélie, Louis Martin, Thérèse,
strengthen our families.

David Bellusci

Roman Cemetery

Sparrows chant, visit their noble
tombs, music in stones, Latin
inscriptions. Family plaques—and plots,
Requiem æternam dona eis
Spruce—furs, pray in rows,
touch a veiled blue sky.
In cracked pots fresh flowers,
rows of violets, white carnations:
still.
Cool November wind blows
across cryptic silence.
Chant has stopped.
Isolated chirps, wings gracefully
flutter on tree-tops. Massive
marble walls contain stories
and secrets—suffering
and forgiveness.
Priests and religious keep their chapels
shrines of remembrance—
prayer. Central Cross, candles
and flowers offered.
Military memorial meditation:
    Strenuis Christi Lux.

Rome: All Saints

Bronze bells ring, eastern sun sings
November Gloria. Faithful flock
through iron gates
hats and habits, veils and suits.
Red light—signal. Confession,
ceaseless shriving, cleansed hearts.
Minds pure.
Timely scent, candles in procession,
chant of angels, open Basilica doors.
Saint John writes, eternal banquet.
Beatitudes invite a laborious
ascent: grazing, stuck
in cracked rock. Courage.
Sweaty skin, vertical climb.
Don't look down—or back.
Blessed be *Agape:*
Frankincense we offer, knees bending—
in Heaven head on ground—
Chants to the Paschal Lamb.
Priest's fingers feed one by one.
   Red stones burn, dove feathers rise:
      vision of Paradise.

Ponte Sant'Angelo by Night

Nighttime *passeggiata**
to the Tiber. November.
Skyness dark. Coldness thick.
Bridge silenced.
Seagulls
shriek in pairs—flocks.
Cylinder fortress protected.
Angel holds a spear
faces south. Points west.
Roman river tranquil
reflects dark green
of Vittorio Emanuele lamps.
Santo-Spirito in Sassia,**
Church—hospital occupy
western wall.
Cold wet rains contained
in granite cracks.
Profile of angels
eternally guard.
I inhale
the Night.

*stroll
***Holy Spirit in Saxony*

First Week of Advent

Pilgrims in winter coats—hats,
Romans process
through solid oak doors.
Esercito—carabinieri—polizia* prepared.
Soldier about nineteen
holds his machine gun,
greets me: *buongiorno.*

Priest and bishop,
Mitres, Roman and Byzantine,
splendor of chasubles sparkle revelation.
Green welcomes purple,
Divine Incarnation in white.
Sweet incense veils Marian mosaics,
bells signal movement forward,
Latin hymn intoxicates faithful.

Confessions and red-light confessionals,
contrite penitents shriven.
God's mercy heard, to conversion,
called. Sin made known.
Judgement anticipated,
soul separated:
hell, or purgatory and heaven.

Christ unites souls
and bodies—
Paradise.

**Military/para-military/police*

David Bellusci

Our Lady of Loreto

Regal
she stands,
a black Madonna,
wrapped in gold ribbons.
Home of the Holy Family,
bricks transported by Angels,
Jerusalem—Adriatic.

A friend prepares
for her reception
novice in Toronto,
Our Lady's order.
Sister from Nairobi
official visit to Rome.

Church filled with soldiers,
Italian Air Force prays
to their patroness.
Time for Confession.
Military in khaki
patrol the alleys.
Swords shield
the passage,
military flags
an arch
leads:
Divine
Altar.

Christmas Colors in Rome

Italian military protect the piazza—and basilica,
standing with machine guns
cold wet days, prolonged nights.
Rome added blue-uniformed
carabinieri, and local police,
entrance security.
Here pilgrims honor
Mary, worship Jesus, pray at His crib.
The faithful approach Confessors,
seeking forgiveness.
Pilgrims and piety, faith in God's Son,
since Herod's days, disturbed.
Baby Jesus, a threat. Have we
not forgotten the Christians
in Syria? The Churches in Iraq?
The Crosses in Lebanon?
Persecuted. Rejected. Abandoned.
Rome a city of pilgrims, resembles
Jerusalem: soldiers to protect believers,
who worship the Prince of Peace.
Across the Mediterranean,
bullets and bombs land dangerously close.
We celebrate your birth, O Lord,
and you only ask conversion
to Truth.

Nativity in Rome

Angels spread their wings, saints
stand below the bell tower
announce
birth of the Christ Child.
Eastern sun illuminates the baroque façade:
stained glass windows narrate history,
wide-open oak doors unveil
the Manger.
Wood
slabs hold the Innocent Lamb.
Armed soldiers patrol the grounds,
devout pilgrims line—push—
to pay homage to God
made Incarnate
from the flesh of AVE.
Nobody enters the House of God
without proper inspection.
And further cleansing,
faithful respond to Grace,
made Righteous,
before God.

Jubilee Year of Mercy, 2015

Opening the Holy Door

Swiss Guard gold red blue,
Bishops, Canons, Confessors,

we wait:

Pope Francis appears, prays
at the *Porta Santa*, Door of Mercy,
we walk through, touch bronze,
Sign of the Cross.

In procession:

cameras flash, digital clicks,
lens zoom, record.

Basilica seats, ticketed lay and religious,
habits black, brown, grey, white,
black suits and dresses,
guests of honour, ambassadors,
Order of Malta, *gendarmerie*.

His Holiness on the papal throne,
Latin hymns to Mary—
prayers to God's Mother.
We profess our Creed, Scriptures read,
Pope's homily on Mercy.

We shout thrice: *Salve, Madre di Dio!**

David Bellusci

Guards kneel, swords forward,
Host and Chalice raised.
We consume the Body and Blood
of Christ, surrounded by saints,
life of Mary in mosaic,
Wood of the Crib in the crypt below.

Jubilee Year of Mercy,
Santa Maria Maggiore, January 1, 2016

*Hail Mother of God!

Prayer of a Confessor

My mission united to Rome begins
    remembering your Sorrow.

My presence in your care
O Mother

to anoint the wounds of the fallen
to offer
    Misericordes sicut Pater.

Before you I kneel,
    Salus Populi Romani:

Write me words of hope,
    so your children do not despair;

Write me words of good counsel,
    so your children grow in sanctity;

Write me words of mercy,
    so your children know the Father's love.

Write me words of wisdom,
    so your children live in the Spirit.

Write me words of faith,
    so your children hear
        the call of Christ
        and prepare for Eternal Life.

David Bellusci

Confession

Sundays I listen to the Latin credo
      uniting Christ's flock
      in His earthly kingdom.

Heaven intoxicates me like a red
wine, offering blessed with frankincense.

         Sins shriven stony hearts caressed.

Cleansed with the words and sign.

         Process towards the
Altar of Sacrifice. Body of worship:

Saints triumphant, communion
of prayers, martyrs in blood,
monks in ecstasy, Christ's soldiers
and sheep.

         Victorious battle cry,
     rewarded with slaughter.

     Angels cry, celestial melodies.

Paradise unlocked: Grace opens
      the narrow gate.

Adolescent Cry

Words cut the heart
with scissors
shape of a child, you tell me
your story…play turns
painful, your hurt driven
by pleasure—family…
friends…games
you cannot end the feeling.
You set your heart
on the *Madonnina*,* begging her
help. Your tired body—marked soul—
merry-go-round
without end.
Your tears not enough to wash
the marks. *Madonnina* takes you
in her arms
she holds your torn body,
to gently stitch your wounds
heart sewn in fine thread.

With sacred oil I anoint you.

**Virgin Mary*

Santa Maria della Vittoria: Chapter 29*

Love quenched in your dreamy eyes,
ocean waves fold your immaculate
dress, divine layers rise to God.
Body elevated, delicate fingers
rest in celestial clouds.
Purified.
Months searching in a desert.
Fasts. Cloister.
Seraphim aims the golden arrow.
Love.
Created in the image
of God, a fallen creature
recreated, redeemed, restored
called:
Conversion.
Communion.
Approach the Altar of God.
Sacrifice: eternal Body, Blood,
remember the everlasting
Covenant fulfilled.
Angel's arrow pierces only once.

*Sculpture of St. Teresa of Avila in Ecstasy,
Church of Our Lady of Victory, Rome
(Gian Lorenzo Bernini, 1598-1690)*

Metaphysics of Divine Love

Nothingness of who I am
is greatest self-knowledge.
God is First Being
is truly great wisdom.
>God is Truth.
>God is Good.
>God is One.

My being has its source in God.
God gives life and takes life.
Source of goodness, God is love.
God creates out of love.
God gives life and takes life
because He loves us.
God calls us into communion
with Him. Holy Communion.
He gives us life in this world,
to prepare us for the world to come
by His grace
> to ascend to Truth

to choose acts of Love
> to accept His call to holiness.

God the Father reaches out to us
sending His Son
offering us eternal life. To embrace
Jesus we receive God's Spirit.
I cannot embrace Jesus if
> my intelligence errs
> my heart is divided
> my soul is unclean.

Holy Reconciliation:

Jesus, purify my intelligence.
Jesus, heal my heart.
Jesus, cleanse my soul
so that I belong only to you,
Jesus my Saviour my God.
And receiving your Body and Blood
    I am in Communion
      with Father + Son + Holy Spirit:
          way to Eternal Life.

Condolences in Lucera

January in Puglia, Adriatic
coast. Snow banks surface:
        unusual sight. Foggia.
Winter coats—gloves and scarf,
cool connection to Lucera,
ticket and one minute to catch
il trenino.*

My cousin's wife greets me
in her superb Lucerino dialect.
Her son smiles, second cousin kisses,
        first time encounter—
        looks like his father.

Chatting in a chilly house, kitchen
oven welcomed. Calls
the *frattello*** in London.

I visit another *cugino* where my aunt
now lives:
        her husband—my *zio*—just died.
Sitting by the fire, logs burn,
light reddens, heat thickens.

        Kisses of condolence.

        I observe family—I never met...

David Bellusci

My cousin's wife prepares late dinner,
> basil, tomatoes, and garlic
> coat the kitchen.
> Paradox of kebab and Sveva mineral water
> on the eastern Adriatic dinner table.
> An unfamiliar cousin greets me—
>> newlywed…

Icy sheets keep me awake—stony city.

Café latte with cornetto at dawn.

Some relatives assemble,
> after morning prayer.

I talk to the *parrocco*,***
> Mass for my *zio's* soul.

Chiacchiaratte**** in the market
made of pickups, trucks, and stands.
Fruit and vegetables shouted.
> Nothing has changed—*really*,

> except duck feather coats.

Holy Door—at the Cathedral
erected over a church-mosque, French Gothic
in southern Italy:
> *La Madonna della Vittoria******
> Anjou victory, Hohenstaufen defeat.

Crowns in conflict!

Lucera's Cathedral (Foggia), Italy, was dedicated to the Assumption of Mary in the 14th century.

*local train
** frattello: brother / cugino: cousin / zio: uncle
***parish priest
****chatter
*****Our Lady of Victory

Byzantine Tower*

Copula decorates the *Daunian*** village
cut in south Adriatic colours—yellow-blue-green.
Cylinder tower stands
silent like a night guard:
carrier of stories,
messages and secrets.
Cobblestone road connects
to *Chiesa dell'Assunta*****—and Byzantium.

Village crossroads and crossfires,
Charles, Frederick, Rome West,
—and Roman Empire East.
Painted in her chapel
next to San Donato's statue
sewn on festive banners, Our Lady of Constantinople
street name, first name, Constans,
Constantine, Constantina.

Extension of *Capitanata*****—Foggian capital.

Smell of wet bricks, daytime moisture
stairways down the tower,
emperor's tunnel—emergency exit.

Twelfth century tower in Biccari (Foggia), Italy
**Foggia region in southern Italy*
***Church of the Assumption*
****Byzantine administrative center*

Madonna della Sanità (Our Lady of Health)*

Shaped as a heart, the village consoles
a valley hidden,
church steeple from afar
echoing narrow roads
Mamma's home.

She sings the hymn as we
approach.

—where she once lived

under stone archways walking
to *zia's*** house on a hill.

May candles lit to honor Mary
zia could not join the procession,
bronchitis breaks her body

with Mamma she waits at her window
for Mary's faithful greeting

—incense—cross—candles—
altar boys in white and red,
a glimpse of the Blessed Mother
—at last—she stops!

to bless Mamma and *zia*
one last time.

*Volturara Appula (Foggia), Italy, 1ˢᵗ Sunday in May
**auntie's*

David Bellusci

Bolsena's Miracle

Cloudy road, tunnels, *Appenini**
birch and oak line green hills.

Cobblestones pave the village
route, Roman and Medieval,
fused.
        Church decorated in layers:
        remnants of catacombs
        devotion to a martyr,
            torturous death,
            renouncing

        pagan
                marriage

        father's match refused.

        Christ her true spouse,
        united in sacrifice: Saint Cristina

Pilgrims pray on their knees,
hostel protects them.

Bohemian priest
    makes his journey
    seeks faith
    celebrates Mass—in doubt.

        Eucharistic blood drips!
        Stones stained!

Urban IV orders liturgy—
    Saint Thomas writes prayers and hymns,
        Adoro Te, perhaps?

    City of Orvieto processions...

        act of Faith.

            *mountain range in central Italy

Joy in Bologna

Cappuccio and cornetto
>*Viale Pietramellara,*
by FS (Ferrovie dello Stato),*
breakfast.

Mediaeval towers claim the city,
defense—wealth. Neptune hides.
Cattedrale San Pietro, Holy Door
and Confession (Mass celebrated, six a.m.)

Basilica San Petronio, half-dressed,
—waiting.
Italian Gothic unveiled.
>Prayers for ignored, forgotten,
>persecuted Christians.

Anxiety: "Obedience!"
>meeting with him—
>*pranzo*** and gelato.
Casual conversation,
>San Tomaso residence,
>fraternal exchanges:

I prayed before the relics
of Father Dominic,
>thanksgiving Mass seven
>years back…

Unexpected reunion,
> racing car print t-shirt,
> cream boardshorts,
almost never recognised him:
> student in Pisa
> professor in Paris.

Brings me to *Basilica Santa Maria Dei Servi.****

Salsiccia pizza and San Pelegrino at *cena.*****

Bologna Centrale: 21:25 departure,
> *abbraccio* and *arrivederci.******

800th Iubilaeum, Bononiae (Bologna) 2016

> > > **Italian State Railways*
> > > ***Italian lunch*
> > > ****Basilica of the Servite Order*
> > > *****supper*
> > > ******hug/goodbye*

Finnish Footsteps in Rome

His way from Helsinki to Rome,
once cloaked by Luther,
now unlocked
by the Keys of St. Peter.

Alexander III's mission:
conversion.

Stones of churches, removed
unearthing relics
twelfth-century Gothic
columns, saints, altars
five hundred years
of monks and nuns, Rome and liturgy
collapse.

No questions asked, no documents
to read, history forgotten,
ignored, erased.

Finland's God:
Made in Saxony.

Saint Henry's relics remain, faithful
pray and venerate,
cathedral built for martyr and bishop.

…

We hear fountains, Borghese Gardens,
red azaleas and chrysanthemum
like wall hangings displayed.

Queen Christina of Sweden joins us
on our *passeggiata*.* Her heroic journey
the Queen offers her crown.
Before me the great mystic
St. Bridget declares promises,
eternity secured by Christ.

I drink running water, cool, endless,
salus. Majestic villa stands
unchanged Roman hands,
Rafaello's green and blue,
Bernini's white marble.

A Nordic seminarian in Rome,
reclaiming his religion, the torch
now lit, to bring light back
to the long days of darkness.

Whisper between umbrella maples,
full moon appears.

Gallerie Borghese, Gardens in Rome

(evening) stroll

David Bellusci

Closure of a Roman Summer

Morning breeze enters my room—
angels breathing. Buzz of Sunday traffic,
soft. The basilica lights turn off, darkness
dispelled by morning light. Regal
column crowned Virgin holds
her crowned Son. Edges
of the crescent moon, above she rises.

Santa Maria Maggiore's bell tower,
Paolina and Sistine copulas reaffirm.
Italian military stand on guard
hold machine guns—all night shift—
others in the army truck.

Walk across Via Merulana, canopy
of shady trees. Cutlery clinking, cappuccino steam,
and coffee pours at Cottini Bar.

I face Basilica Santa Prassede
where relics are kept of the Cross.

Down the cobblestone street
smell of fresh bread, orders
of *parmigiano, genova, san Daniele,**
and olive oil.
Staff voices, clients chatting,
Buona giornata…grazie**…

At the Mercenate tower, the nuns live,
between Carmelites and Augustinians
as cloistered neighbours.
Prayers continue like endless incense.

My last summer Mass.

> *cheese and brands of cold cut meats
> **good day/thank you

Blessed Pier Giorgio Collection

Prayers on a Holy Mountain

I kneel before Our Lady
        ancient Oropa Sanctuary
        Eusebian origins.

Holy Door:
              Day of Indulgence,
              Year of Mercy.

Olive Rosary beads

    smooth between fingers.

Mass concelebrated.

Salve Regina.
Mary blesses our syllables.

Bright painting of Blessed
Pier Giorgio:
        Borghese in suit & tie,
        flowers, petitions,
        for his *Madonna*.

Thoughts of you in winter
                dampness.
I hear my footsteps,
    along the Oropa stream,
uphill, icy clouds: your smile.

Church bells pierce the sky,
        hope for a fragile world.
        Mount Mucrone stands at a distance.

Pray for us, Pier Giorgio.

Presentation, February 2016, Oropa (Biella), Italy

Silence of Oropa

You hear the owls at night,
        stars still over mountains,

sun beams through morning mist

and bare beech trees point—
                Biella far in mist.

Mt. Mucrone northwest,
        massive rocks,
        majestic copula.

Below *La Madonna Bruna* waits
in her ancient sacellum:
                she listens.

Columns follow Arduzzi's
cloister, Sabaudian insignias.

Voices crack thick silence.

Winds return at dusk
        blow into corridors
               rattling doors.

Rows of *ex-votos*
mark Mary's intercession.

        Bells chant:
           prayer.

Hills of Beauty

I journey from Favaro to Pollone
as an April pilgrim.
Guiding me, the range of snow-capped Alps.
Gracefully descending, green furs
and pine, gardens of budding trees.
Cattle bells and rooster melodies
repeat like a chorus, swallows
join with their endless songs. Brook flows
from boulders to rocks, meandering
down the hills.
Pier Giorgio walked to Oropa
early in the morning to pray the Rosary
and receive Holy Communion.
Beauty, he gazed upon from mountains
to the shrine where the Virgin Mary stands.
Beauty of Divine Creation cleansed
his heart and mind, opening Pier Giorgio's
soul to receive the Gifts
God planned for Him. And Pier Giorgio
nodded,
    Yes: Truth, Love, Eternal God.

My Oropa Cell

Four walls,
Crucifix, picture of *La Vergine Bruna**
creaky birch-wood floor as I pace.
Window panel opens
to eight frames.
White clouds push over the Alps.
Blue sky—hidden—re-appears.
Jagged rocks, massive granite
chiseled. Spring trees in blossom approach me.
Stream of water falls over rocks, chatters
throughout the day, as if my companion.
Yellow shrike gracefully lands on a brick
rooftop. Clouds shift south, sunlight eclipsed.
I withdraw from my defined space
and pray in the Old Basilica
before Our Lady, alone.
In her blue cape and red robe, she holds Jesus
with her left arm, a green apple with a Cross in her right.
Attentive she listens. My eyes fixed
on her. Silence between us.
I return to my cell.
And wait.

*Black Virgin

Below Mount Mucrone

Cappuccino and milk chocolate warm me
—energy. Mineral water for my ongoing
headaches. Italian flag waves, *düvert*,
bar door, Piemontese,
besides *aperto* and *opened*.
I lie at the foot of Mount Mucrone
lake frozen at 1900 meters in mid-April.
Crucifix and altar erected by Alpinini pilgrims.
Gush of water, music of sparrow fills
the sacred space. I participate by offering
prayers to Our Lady, my rhythmic litany.
Snow-like diamonds sparkle. Mucrone,
Pier Giorgio observed from his Pollone room.
Blue skies on a sunny day, an invitation to climb
—explore God's creation. Intoxicated by nectar,
rock and snow lie beside me as faithful
companions. Mountain climbing—
Blessed Pier Giorgio—
Easter Triduum—
Penance—Eucharist—Resurrection.

David Bellusci

Kneeling Before You

I pray at your feet, Madonna of Oropa
apple and leaf
requests of hearts troubled—confused,
seeking you, O Black Virgin, Strength:
                              Silence:
                              Peace:
Grey clouds, thick, settle
over the rocky valley.
Mountains magnificent,
layered in white:
                Mount Mucrone looks over.
Healing me, God's Mother offers me
the cure:
        Sacrificial Mass,
Mother of Our Savior directs me.
My restless night
                awake since midnight,
                asleep at five a.m.
God remains present, the Madonna
draws me to her mantle.
In my rawness, I battle:
                I wrestle
with solitude
with God.
Signs barely audible, sounds
of God's voice penetrate
when I am stripped…

Lunch by the "Ruscello"*

From Lake Mucrone a current runs
down the mountain. Granite rocks crushed.
Splashes of spring melts snow…
thick rain. Italian Alps,
Mount Mucrone stands in majesty.
Snow outlines sharp and wide
—peaks. Brick houses serve as *trattoria*,**
produce goat cheese and honey, farmers
welcome pilgrims.
Panini—*prosciutto cotto* and *magagna*,
bottle of *aqua frizzente*…
my mind returns to yesterday's *polenta concia*.***
Pier Giorgio who mentions the *Biellese*****
dish in his letters. *Did he sit here and meditate?*
Blossoms on birch trees hang over the river
to stretch and absorb afternoon sun—
stop for bumble bees.
Street Chapel of St. Eusebius overlooks
the road.
Here Our Lady is Queen.

*stream
**restaurant
***cornmeal and fondina
****Provincial city where Oropa is situated

David Bellusci

April 6th: Praying with Blessed Pier Giorgio

Crucifix on the wall, I recognize
as the gift
—surprise for your sister on her wedding day.
She wondered about this gesture,
having opened
your box,
the ivory body crucified.
Our Savior
with his arms outstretched, nailed. Gift
of God's Son to the world.
You understand love's purpose.
The gift you offer
to a person whom you love—your dearest sister:
the Gift of salvation.
The suitability of a Crucifix as a wedding gift,
you seized the meaning of love and gift.

…

Your portrait, taken
on your death bed—
or rather,
birth into eternity: beauty of holiness—
in life and death.
You lived, embracing beauty
of sea and the mountain, leading your gaze
to the beautiful Mother of God.
Beauty surrounded you,
and you penetrated
beauty with your heart and soul to encounter

the author of Beauty: Creator God.
The white & black photo—your
approach to life: things were true or false,
good or evil, yes or no.
Beauty in honesty.
…

The balcony doors open
to the foretaste
of paradise: blue sky, snow-layered Alps,
green of pines, white blossom.
Flowers
you offered to Jesus and Our Lady.
You are united with them:
pull us up with you and the saints,
tie us with your
cord, as on the Alps,
help us not to fall,
but to choose virtue, to make sacrifices, to look
upward, courageously,
with your help, and Our Lady,
the saints, focused on Christ—
for Eternity.

Pollone (Biella), Italy, 2016

Breath of Time (Night before leaving Oropa)

Pine trees
shades of green
mountain tops—a stream.
Needles, leaves, and blossoms waltz
in the alpine wind.
Water falls over rocks.
Silence.
Clouds hover, hang motionless
or float
almost secretly
as if they hide time.
Blue remains unchanged, soft pastel,
darkened sky signals time—night.
Silence unveils change.
Church bells announce: silence.
To act, except to meditate, robs me of time.
Stillness outside, and in, while time is still, still.
My heart beats.
My thoughts anticipate darkness
as if I have not savoured time.
Night teases me
because I cannot be sure of the following day.
Sublime beauty of night
disturbs.
Sky coated in stars
I am tormented
because darkness places me
in time:

> I breathe, wait for the light of dawn…

April 18, 2016

Read at the Blue Met Literary Festival,
Montreal, April 30, 2017. Modified from the original.

Pilgrim Gates

Sacred Soil

Sacred vessels withstand time
blood and spirit, jewel-crossed lands.
Your queen processed through the waters
even the Blue Nile bows to your wonders.
Scorching sands afar,
seduce nomadic wanderers
veiled entourage, tempting date palms
gushing falls, sword and creed.
Monks paddle, heads covered, God's chosen
ones. Somewhere the Ark of the Covenant
is hidden.
I found my way as a mission teacher
my father a soldier swept away.
Stories of your glory,
silent treasures, ancient secrets. His team
engineered the road from Addis Ababa.
In the nineties* I probed your soul
—threatened by those who do not know your Mother.
Battles of splattered blood.
Your monks
disappear…and the world remains silent.
Are your rulers
kings and queens? Or strangers? Sheba
left her rose petals
for you to kiss,
her lilac-scented oils to smell.

My father praised you—
              and dreamed about you…

Lake Tana, Ethiopia
        *Beating the Drums (Mambo Press, 1997)

Nuns of Rweza

Morning light streams across the church
nuns in white habits and black veils,
two novices wear white.

Lauds, time to praise,
sun spins through the narrow windows.

Their hands raise in union and chant
elderly nun reads the Scriptures
in her weak voice.
Her poor vision makes words inaudible.
Cantor intones, drum beats…
They return to pray one last time,
dark church using sun-powered light
Kirundi syllables heard, bodies move.

Doors locked, nuns pray
in a violent world.

Fearless, alone in a cloister,
in distant hills that offer peace.
Bloodshed witnessed—
bow before God,
trust in the Almighty Creator,
God of Redemption and
Everlasting life.
In daylight the birds sing.
Butterflies leave their marks.
Pineapples, papaya, and mango
stretch across the field.

David Bellusci

Young men, boys perhaps, pray
silently, seeking Truth, the Way.
Quietly they cut bread, pour water,
and chew on sweet potatoes and rice.
Darkness repeats.

In daytime hours they appear
with food…and water.

The brick cloistered walls separate
and protect
sacred from the profane.

Rweza, Burundi

At Carmel

On university grounds
we contemplate:
not the career of a Computer Scientist
or a Linguist doing field work,
but the majesty of God,
calling upon angels and saints.
We exchange mystics with late night chai.
She works to support her brother
somewhere in Africa.
She takes off her black leather skirt and blouse
to put on the brown habit and white cape
of Carmel.
I joined the prioress and nuns
in prayer, offering classes
on Truth and Love:

I became their student.

Masses celebrated
the prioress observed me
in my line of vision, her eyes set
on God's Altar.
United with them at five-thirty
when the birds
have commenced their morning lauds,
I hear them process.
Together—before God we kneel.
Our classes follow with questions
and reflection. They are my cloistered
teachers silently

explaining *agape*.
They seized life's essence, true meaning
of Genesis and Revelations, the worship
of the sacrificed Lamb,
love perfected.
Anticipated.

August 2009 — First Masses

Nervous, I ascended the regal stairs
kissed the splendid altar
being unworthy of the task.
St. Dominic from above in perfect glory.
Crucifix before me, the words I prayed
in honor of the Assumption.
Sweating, I trembled, jubilant,
I stood, I bowed, I kneeled,
his relics assured me of his approval,
the words I said, with water and wine,
real presence no one could deny
overwhelmed me in Bologna.

The chapel was ready,
her solemn feast I could celebrate
before her skull. Precious relic!
How could it be?
The prayers of her solemn day I pronounced,
April readings in August.
Cold beads dripped from my forehead
down my back, as I bowed
reading the Canon of the Saints.
Mamma and Papa always in my prayers
and all those seeking intercession.
Two candles give light to a darkened room
from centuries of smoke and pilgrim visits.
As I look at you, St. Catherine,
I feel my tears. I never thought I could
be so close. And here we pray:
you and I to *Sweet Jesus*.

Andrea helps me with the amice
I wore only once before.
He offers me an alb.
Another altar boy assists me
with the white chasuble.
Andrea leads the way, holds
the cruets of water and wine
I wonder where I would say Mass.
He looks for a vacant altar
and walks across the nave
to the altar of Our Lady of Succor.
The Maltese boy stands to my right,
as I prepare the Missal and readings.
I kiss the altar,
look above to the Crucifix,
feel my body tremble before God.
Andrea responds to the prayers.
Water trickles down my eyebrows
down my back as I read through the
Roman Canon.
Christ is present. I bow. Andrea kneels.
I consume the precious Body and Blood
and turn to the twelve-year-old who receives
Jesus on his tongue.
On just an ordinary Thursday morning,
I entered solemn eternity.

Bologna, Saint Dominic's Basilica
Siena, Saint Dominic's Basilica
Rome, Saint Peter's Basilica, Altar of Our Lady of Succor

Poem for Our Blessed Lady*

December snow falls
in dawn silence
each flake a white rose petal,
offered to Mary, Dominican
Rosary beads, St. Alphonse's praises.
Virgin purity, chosen, privileged
by grace.
Before you I kneel in morning prayer.
You struck a medal,
I wear in your honor,
enveloped by your mantle of love,
graces you obtain for me.
The purity of your flesh
is
the Tabernacle of my saving God.
Trusting children
filled with hope
God directs upon my path,
help me
help them.
Melt our hearts with your
tender love. Lead us all to your divine Son.
His merciful heart beats for us,
He waits.
His hands outstretched:
Divine embrace
for all eternity.

*First published in the B.C. Catholic,
Vancouver, British Columbia, 2013*

David Bellusci

Grotto in Shepherd's Field*

Judean breeze fills a December night
countless stars designed for heaven
olive branches repeat their dirge.
Incense of farm animals and hay,
Mother embraces her newborn babe,
a lullaby of adoration.
Her husband from David's House,
holds a vigil lamp, protects,
invites, watches over.
I fall on my knees: love submits to truth.
My mind knows.
My heart desires.

You, O Lord.

Your eyes set on your Mother.
Her flesh, your flesh.
Without stain. Without mark.
Immaculate.
But I see fear in your infant eyes,
images of whips, and thorns,
nails. Falling sandals…
you discover your mission,
you run into your mother's arms.
She wraps her body around you
on the Cross

Son of God.

Shepherd's Field, Bethlehem, Holy Land, June 2010

**First published in the B.C. Catholic,
Vancouver, British Columbia, 2014*

Clothed in White

Pilgrim led: thirsts to know Father's will.
    Mary calls, invitation:
        listening…

    Remote village,
        on rainy days jagged rocks slippery,
        glorious days of sunshine.

    She stands so splendid in white:
    gentle hand motions forward,
    hours of line-ups for Confession—

        open hearts, wounds deep
            cuts…

    Word heals, Cross anoints.

Pious men in coarse brown tunics testify—
    their mission:
        providential, miraculous.

In front of St. James a woman kneels
in prayer. I read the Scriptures
in the morning breeze and sweet Italian
syllables of *Ave Maria*.

Cross on a hill, majestic climb,
    scapular stuck in stones,
        sandals tattered.

David Bellusci

Youthful pilgrims, silent company,
stop at the fourth
mystery dedicated to priests…
$$\text{love fills our hearts.}$$

Evening sole dinner, Croatian wine,
tomorrow feasting Corpus Christi.

Mir.*

*Peace

Medjugorje, Bosnia-Herzegovina, Wednesday, June 6, 2012

Roman Setting

Roman sun sets, the silhouette
of a basilica,
steeple, cupola, Mary on a pillar.
Benedict XIV, no Renaissance Pope,
his inscription. Angels hold shields, Cross pierces
a blue sky. Columns solid. Gold leaf first
from Spain, Isabella the Catholic,
and Alexander VI leave their sign:
castrated bull.
Paolina chapel remembers the Borghese,
and she *"salvus"* of the Romans.
King David
crowned with white marble.
Confessionals with red lights
men listen in white habits.
Byzantine mosaics, story of Jesus.
Miraculous snow falls in Rome,
Pope Liberius dedicates the site to Mary.
Same beggar waits outside
a silver-tooth Gypsy, sometimes
his wife helps hand empty, holds a photo
with children.
Pigeons land by the fountain where daytime tourists
are replaced by nighttime party-makers.
Romans escape to the beaches.
Only the marble saints remain
to narrate history…

Clear sound rings through the piazza,
bell strikes…nine, *la sperduta.**

*the lost girl

Capes and Hoods

Silence, the Venetian lagoon at night
demands. One-time university
friendships bonding in the name of
Plato, Aristotle, and God.
Monastery
or City.
Monk or
Politician.
Patricians Contarini, Giustiniani—all.
Departures and deaths,
the cloister
odor of fasts, a procession
of black tunics in lighted candles
evening prayers.
Sunset on cemetery island.
I hear requests as I leave the boat,
I see the iron doors open.
The lion's flame envelopes me.
Waiting for a discourse on "love":
San Michele where the monks prayed
and their cells of strict observance,
not all joined,
a wave of radicals stuck to the city,
claiming God outside cloister
walls.
Only the columns remain.

Cause of Our Joy – "La Gritería"*

And the Bishop cried out into the crowd:

Who is the cause of our joy?

Excited people replied
in one booming voice, one loving cry:

The Immaculate Conception of Mary!

Firecrackers cracked
right through the square
fireworks blasted into the dark
purple and yellow in the sky.
Striped *gigentos* and bright *gigentas*
twisted and turned
to a Marian beat:
Bishop's cry of joy.

Heavy drums banged, to more *alegria.***
Six p.m. Angelus: *La Purísima****!
Fiesta faces, Mary's the infinite cause.
He incenses the woman in blue and white,
she welcomes her children waving below.

Sing and dance, one family.
One heart celebrates the Most Pure One,
Oh, Holy Mother of God.

December 7, León, Nicaragua

*the shouting
**joy
***Most pure one

David Bellusci

"La Purísima" (Most Pure One)

Altar for Mary, a Nicaraguan home
songs dedicated to the Immaculate,
make music with shakers and tambourines.
Containers of delights, sandwich,
sweets, desserts, chips, sugar cane, drinks.
Statues of Mary, Jesus, and Cross,
poor—rich, men—women
young—old, all invited to
Mary's motherly love. No child
excluded.
Boys exercise their voices, shy girls help.
All her children learn the lyrics:
L'Iglesia sin Maria todavía no es Iglesia!
"A Church without Mary is not yet a Church!"
Novena prayers—not mere devotion—
lead to Christ.
Shakers shake. Tambourines jangle.
Fireworks crack and light.
Smiles extend
across room-made-chapel,
hostess and family delight to share God's
goodness. Day four of the Novena.

*"*The Most Pure One": title given to the Blessed Virgin Mary.
Novena devotion in Nicaragua in honour
of the Immaculate Conception
observed November 29–December 7.*

Nicaragua Nuns

Nuns seated gracefully in a row
pen and paper, some with a Bible.
White habits, white veils, ears covered,
we pray.
Introduce ourselves,
        Nicaragua, Costa Rica, El Salvador,
          and Mexicans for the Managua foundation,
            community of ten monjas.*
In morning breeze, pleased to reflect,
grow together, journey to Truth.
Eyes express eagerness
to listen, follow their patron,
and mystic patroness: Holy Spirit source.
Nuns inquire, sweetness of radiant light.
Eyes reveal theme: purity of love.
Afternoon heat visits. Winds whip.
        Our Lady of the Rosary
              holds Baby Jesus
      Saint Dominic and Saint Catherine
            kneel
    enclosure separates us.
Black hands tick minutes—
            life consecrated.

nuns

David Bellusci

My Fifth Year

In May I knelt before you
in Nazareth
praying hymns of love
my Mother Immaculate
candles lit in a stone chapel
Byzantine mosaic walls, Crusader arches.
Your lily fragrance purifies
your battle attire protects and crushes.
In Rome before *Salus populi*
Romani I consecrated myself
to you, Mother of God
united hearts beat together:
truth and love.
December returns and I celebrate
your Immaculate Conception
in a Nicaraguan Basilica:
protect me, keep me
in God's grace,
faithful to Christ's Vicar
and His Church
keep me pure, help me in holiness,
let Christ live in me.

December 8, 2014, Managua, Nicaragua
Year of Consecrated Life

Morning in Prague

Vltava River waves into the Czech sun
St. Vito Cathedral stands
in coronation splendor
solid stone—royal throne.
Elected government
now affirms white-red
and blue-triangle—
identity held centuries
before Huss.
Charles's bridge recalls triumphant saints,
Latin inscription of one faith.
French-Austrian marriages produce
Rudolph, pride of Praha. *Where
is your heir?* For the Holy Empire?
Modern sculptor
of a burned heretic in a Baroque square
out of place, out of time. Faithful
Saint Agnes the Bohemian canonized
—and the communist state collapsed.
Will you return to God?
I listen to Prague's morning sparrows
by the Faculty of Theology
where celibate seminarians quietly
walk the Roman corridors.
A pilgrim offers
me white lilies to inhale the fresh
scent, sweet.
Dressed in divine glory,
we kneel before the Infant Jesus
of Prague.

David Bellusci

Finding Warsaw

Scaffolds rise, dark windows
draped in fabric clouds.
A woman turns to a priest for work—
church built, unfinished bricks
income for a poor family, she prays.
Seventeenth-century capital
flattened, barbed wire
replaces wooden fences. Remnants
of Nazis. Relics of Marx. Tyrannies
imposed.
In a green park Chopin performs
—theatre where the king stands
in his playground island—
eternal entertainment
ball after ball.
Is it the mermaid swimming? Why is
the ancient cathedral so somber?
Resistance to the Vasa Kings
—third column stands.
Heathens mock religious rites,
common language ridiculed.
Only the ta-ta-ta of slaughter
can be heard.
Or is it that silenced
martyr drowned* by hate that sunk
Warsaw?

*In October of 1984, Polish Roman
Catholic priest, Jerzy Popieluszko,
was kidnapped and killed by Communists.

Kneeling in Częstochowa*

A painting of Saint Anthony brightens
the wall of her rural home in Głogowiec.
Her younger siblings rely on their sister,
she still remembers God's voice.
At Kraków the young woman unemployed
visits St. James Church turning to the priest.
She prays, kneeling before Our Lady
at Czestochowa, entrusting her life to her
Holy Queen. Now a novice at Łagiewniki
divine messages of mercy.

He offers himself as a child, loving Mary,
for the Virgin, martyrdom and purity.
Częstochowa shapes his Marian vocation,
chant of evening prayer, the icon veiled.
Studying in Rome he serves the Church,
knight's militia begins, Niepokalanów
proclaims the Immaculate. In Nagasaki
spared, his mission moves to Auschwitz.
Surprising Nazis and prisoners who watched,
he offers his blood—mercy for a stranger.

His father taught the best of religion,
a humble Wadowice home, career
in drama chosen. Mother, brother, father
deceased, praying before his Queen
at Częstochowa, recognises the seminary.
Hides from godless systems—religion punished.
Teaching ethics in Lublin, prepares for Krakow,
call to Rome. Mary dodges the bullets, Fatima

David Bellusci

intervenes, proof at Zakopane. Forgiving the killer, love sheds blood, God's mercy.

Częstochowa, Poland, May 2015

*First published in the B.C. Catholic, Vancouver, British Columbia, 2015

Mother of Auschwitz

You find yourself in a selection,
process you did not choose.
Armed men, uniformed fear,
you are a victim of choices,
humanity silenced.
You arrive with your luggage,
floral dishes, aluminum pots,
and whatever you carried
across a desert journey of tacks.
Are you a scientific experiment,
probed by science,
shaped by technology?
Heartless investigations ignore
the beating heart.
Where do you go next? You
are either uninformed
or misinformed.
"Systems" militant people
bring to power: sophisticated
structures
to silence.

A young mother silently carries
her son...

David Bellusci

Priest at a Death Camp

A child—Purity and Martyrdom
echo in your heart—White and Red
crown your vocation.
Infused by Grace, you march
to the beat of Courage. In Rome your
footsteps follow ancient bricks and stone;
studies and faith unveil the Trinitarian God
you contemplate.
Protestors, demonstrators, Masons and heretics,
propaganda against God, Christ, His Church.
You put on the armour of Mary's Militia
publish and preach against godless
ideology: Marxists and Nazis.
Truth is not betrayed; trust is being not afraid.
Monastery and Mission, Parish and Believers,
the Immaculate your guide, conversion
to her Divine Son your project.
No continent creates a distance.
No language causes a hindrance.
Christ is your priesthood.
Persecution slams you into a death camp,
barbed wires, injected evil, *Odium fidei*.
You starve and sing hymns to the Immaculate.
Your dark cell smells of death,
Grace makes you fearless.
Fragrance of Mary, the taste of Jesus
open you to Paradise.

White Wine with Anne

Focused on Sacred Scripture
>she appears Tuesday evenings
>like an A-student positioned to listen
>—at the front row:
>>Saint Paul's Letters, Saint John's Gospel,
>>and Genesis—eyes wide open.

Politely she informs me of her absences…
Texas visits in the winter, her farm waits with cattle,
>her Angus Rufus,
>>and catfish.

Anne feeds Rufus chocolate milk—
>he dutifully licks,
>and they moo each other on the phone
>long distance.
>>He keeps the ladies occupied,
>>fills the farm with calves…

Sitting in Piazza San Marco, Anne drinks Pinot Grigio—
her favorite white—we raise our glasses
>>to exquisite Venice…

Pilgrims in Poland,
>Kraków, Katowice,
>Auschwitz:

Anne examines the names of victims
I stand beside her.
>She reads across rows
>>down columns—family members…

Italian restaurant in Toronto, Anne holds her fork
of fettucine, prefers syllables of thought
over noodles, emotions expressed—
>eyes wet:

David Bellusci

    speaks to me of the Messiah
      she longed for…
At a cave where the Hermits of Saint Paul worship
in Budapest,
Mass is celebrated. Anne listens to the Word
and steps forward to receive Him
      the One
       whom she knows.

Jesus Holds a Porcelain Wicker Basket

Your crown is chipped white,
holding Jesus in your arms
at his thigh. He holds a wicker
basket of bread
or fruit to nourish me.
The Infant generously offers,
with open hands to feed.
I am a hungry passerby filled
with desire. A satisfied body feels
no pain of hunger—no reason to stop—
to reach out.
Fruit from a garden once poisoned;
seduced to satisfy.
Banished.
The garden of Jesus and his Mother
an invitation
                to sacred bread
                and new grapes:
                —Eternal Life

David Bellusci

April in Galilee

Winds lash
at the trees,
> palm branches sharp blades
> silent sun
>> pricks.

Vultures fall
in flight,
> endless cries
> sparrows' offer
>> *shalom*
> buried songs

Force builds and whips
solid rock
> disfigured in time
> turn-taking spears, thorny

edges, hide the blue surf.
Tiberius
secretly watches
> ignoring cries of a lamb

under the sun
> sacrificed.

On the Sea of Galilee

Jesus and his disciples
sailed these waters, fishing,
stormy weather, fear of drowning…
Jesus appears:
I pierce the depth of the blue
with a torn heart.
Tears suffer with Jesus,
why bitter?
I desire Communion
with my Lord, and the Cross
is the only way.
Why so long the wait?
Fire burns of love and purgation
—my sins.
Jesus is with me
but I want Him always
inseparable union.

Why the long wait, Lord?

April 25, 2014, Holy Land

Our Lady of Altötting

Quiet—*Stille**—of a wooden chapel
hidden
in monastic fields of Bavaria.

Virgin holds the sceptre—
and Christ Child.
Pilgrims proclaim a journey of love.

Octagon walls covered colored
in true faith—
ex-votos of believers. Drowned boy recovered.

French Houses build with German Clerics.

Josef prayed
before her with pilgrims
of München, and accompanied
the Great Polish Pope and Saint.

On her scepter Benedict's sign
of fidelity.

Lives transformed turning to Mary,
disciples of Jesus.

Holy faith, Holy silence.

Grace painted in healing:
journey calls, journey moves.

Christ heals. Rebirth. Renewed.
Sainthood: offer the offering of self.

I meditate your Beauty.
I am led to your Son, my Savior.

silence

Altötting (Bavaria), Germany, May 2015

Solitudine (Solitude)*

Ocean waves rush in, caressing me;
a lost dog approaches
to smell my feet.
Presence of fishermen, their nets cast,
walk into the water, so distant.
Across the fields palm trees dance,
their countless leaves sizzle.
Thick clouds loom to signal rain:
I smell the sea of the Adriatic coast.

To the raw shores I am directed
alone, naked and crude:
union with unknown blessed.
Solitude
of being—*essence*,
God waits with a multitude.
My journey announced:
I accompanied you in your misery,
you were not alone.

Engines at the bus station I hear,
watching where you sit and wait.
Departure: Three.
Destination: Paradise.
Trust in love; hope in my heart.
Only the Divine quenches this desire:

God embrace me,
touch my soul in endless waves.

*Submitted to XIX "Cala Petralana"
Olbia (Sardegna), Italy, 2015. Modified from the original.

Saluti da Roma* — (Greetings from Rome)

"Buy a postcard of this Roman basilica,
and mail the souvenir home!"

Who will ponder my words across the sea?

Mamma yearns for my punctual cards,
    and writes back in accented syllables.
Papa waits and falls asleep by the phone
    to receive my calls.
Now both chant hymns of angels, beyond
    the clouds. I hear their prayers.

My verses I throw to the sun that caresses
    me when I rise.

To the stars I write letters, they accompany
    me at night.

Ocean waves reflect and reply, never
    exhausted to listen.

The moon consoles me,
    on my meandering routes of oak.

I dip into the wet blue night,
    the velvet ink envelopes me.

    The bones of saints, I kiss.

*First published in *Philadelphia Poets*, 2017

La Vita è Bella — "Life is Beautiful"

Montepulciano, we toast
red bouquet, reflects life in his eyes:
La vita è bella.

      Train draft immobilizes
      three weeks
      of acupuncture follow
      head—shoulders—arms. Unkempt.
      No medication, ulcerated stomach,
      ultrasound finds nothing.
      Steady cold, winds hit hard
      a seventy-five-year-old.

Nestor joins us his *Mensa di Bacco**
recommendations.
All'ammatrice* Elio orders
                —con buccatini.*

      Fabiola knows what *padre* likes,
      her energetic son jokes like mamma.

Elio engages—entertains mother and son.
My request predicted: lasagna *bolognese.*

      Buffala cheese, prosciutto and foccaccia
      placed on white tablecloths:
                —*la vita è bella.*

                *Italian restaurant in Rome
      **All'amatriciana — tomato sauce cooked with bacon
                      ***spaghetti with holes

Wedding Colors

Her head covered in a white veil,
shiny black hair falls to the side. White dress
ankle-length, short sleeves, white
shoes to match, and modest neckline,
reveal her story, who she is.
His powder-blue suit, single-breast,
pastel shirt and matching bow tie,
accentuate his eyes, who he is.
I observe both as each pronounce
solemn words:
> of man and woman
> created by God
> united as one:
> two souls
>> willing to pardon,
>> engage in lifetime love:
>> joy—sacrifice.

Altar of God sanctifies, elevates
natural to supernatural.
He struggles—emotions surface,
she responds—eyes water.
> Each holds the right hand,
> gaze of love: lover-beloved.
>> The gold ring is placed,
>> finger through finger,
>> bond indivisible.

Chieti (Abruzzo), Italy, August 2017

Blessing of Autumn Classes

Fir trees, tall
        slender
        branches bend
in icy wind.

Fern, holly—graciously—
      spread green shades.

Brave squirrel visits,
      shares soggy leaves
      and glares.

Logs wet, neatly stacked,
        scent
        of fresh wood
        fills the air.

Street lamps remain lit.
Rain drizzles
signing the Cross,
made of cedar slabs.

        Mary, Joseph, Jesus
bless

students carrying backpacks.

      Hearts pierced
      by truth:
          sophia's invitation.

St. Nicholas Campus, Langley, British Columbia
Site of Catholic Pacific College, Liberal Arts programme

Mary Mother of God, 2018

Morning fog wraps the city,

scraping
frost
off my Honda windows. Wool
gloves feel too thin,
        my *capuce* tucked
under a black hat.

        Street lights
flicker

green on empty Rupert Street.

Mountains
north hidden,
dawn dispels winter darkness.

The drive takes me to my elementary school
and Church of my baptism.

    …baptistery to the left entering the Church
    apart like catechumens—
    converted space—

    baptismal font in the sanctuary.

Marian blue tiles cloak outdoor walls,
Mary's title
of the Servite Order,

          Scalabrini follow
          tradition stands firm.

Black & white photos, fifty years reveal,
Sisters of Sorrows, Sisters of Halifax

black veils
white wimples and cornettes,

habits their cloister.

I process left: Mary stands since my
First Communion. That Fatima May crowned,
robed in regal red.
We learn to kneel at the Communion rail
where we receive the Body of Christ.

I kneel on the sanctuary prepared
for the *Sanctus* to end
                    step to ring
          the bell.

Jesus-Joseph reassigned—
          Mary's spouse repositioned:
          Tabernacle-side houses Jesus
          —away from altar.

Angelic worship un-altered.

Kneeling, Lenten fasts and Advent
prayers, candles lit in her presence.

I sought guidance, Seat of Wisdom.

First Sorrow, Simeon holds Jesus,
prophesies,
>
> *sword will pierce your soul,*
>
> > yesterday's reading,
> > St. Luke's Holy Family.

Mary, Jesus, and Joseph, Nativity Scene:

> Birth of our Savior.
> Bethlehem Manger.
> City of David. Tribe of Judah.

Excitement stirs my blood,
New Year with God's Mother,
the faithful—family of believers.

Spanish rhythms accompany,
Filipino choir connects joyous smiles.

After Mass
> parents explain they arrived from Fiji,
> their son served Mass.

> I reply to questions, *the Italians lived
> in East Vancouver...*

> Chinese lady remembers
> our September Mass:

>   her boy attends
>   Our Lady of Sorrows, too.

Recessional we sang during the school
Mass repeats:

> *Hail Mary, full of grace…*

Feast of the Presentation at the Benedictine Monastery

Darkness—silence—inhaling
morning frost.

Black habits flutter
robed in choir stalls. David's Psalms,
Malachi's prophecy,
Luke's Simeon and Anne,
mark the Holy Offering…

Bees' wax warms the foyer,
cream-yellow candles fill a wooden box,
coat ledges.
Solemn prayers, Abbot's blessing—
procession we enter the church
seminarians kneel. Gregorian chant
directs hearts and souls.
Cement slabs testify solidity—stability:

Platonic: Aristotelian: Stoic:

>   Abbot stands
>   Father of Benedictines
>   Authority unbroken

His hand raised, we bow our heads:
offering ourselves on Candlemas.

David Bellusci

Mountain Nuns

Holy Saturday
                drive north
Valley Road
Squamish: nation—mountains—river.
Phil Chuk Creek
                  narrow bridge signals
                  monastery hidden beneath
                  Cloudburst mountain.
Majestic blue spring stretches:
        white peaks string
        around the chapel:
                white robes, black veiled
shape silent prayer:
                        chants
                        worship:
Creator God:
Father-Son-Holy Spirit:
Trinitarian graces descend on earth
                  ascend into Eternity.

First Communion

Instruction to prepare her mind and heart
Sacred Scriptures and Catholic Catechism
a seven-year-old educated to distinguish
right and wrong, goodness and wickedness,
choose the path of Communion with God,
confession to the priest, Christ's representative,
to receive her Savior.
Eyes illuminated
like all seven-year-olds at the Banquet.
Children and adults listen attentively to their
priest, the one appointed to take care of souls,
Cura animarum. The Sacrifice offered
children line up, hands folded, boys and girls
wearing Communion suits and dresses.
Each child kneels at the prie-dieu.
"Body of Christ," her eyes fixed, the Eucharist,
she receives Jesus on her tongue: "Amen."
Corpus Christi Sunday for First Communion,
Mass followed by Adoration, all
in Solemn Procession, hymns sung,
mothers, fathers, grandfathers, grandmothers,
brothers, sisters, aunts, uncles, cousins and friends,
form One Body. Together, kneeling, we sing
Tantum Ergo, incense rises—
the foretaste of Heaven.

About the Author

David Bellusci is a priest, philosopher, and poet, who began writing poetry in the 1990s while in France. He was inspired by a lecture on philosophy that led to Rainer Maria Rilke's Letters to a Young Poet. Moved by the pastel colors of the French Loire, and the spiritual intensity of Saint Thérèse of Lisieux's poetry, Bellusci's poetry developed from his religious experiences  in Italy and France, his travel and work across Africa, his teaching in Latin America and India, and his pilgrimages across Europe and the Middle East.

Holding a B.A. in English Literature from the University of Toronto, an M.A. in Linguistics from the University of Calgary, Bellusci completed his M.F.A. in Creative Writing at the University of Nebraska. He obtained both his Licentiate in Theology and Doctorate in Philosophy at the Dominican College in Ottawa. Bellusci's poetry has been published in Australia, Canada, New Zealand, the United Kingdom, and the United States. He has read his poetry in Toronto, Montreal, Nebraska City, and Rome. He is a member of the Catholic Writers Guild, and he teaches philosophy and religious studies at Catholic Pacific College in Langley, British Columbia. David Bellusci lives with his Dominican community in Vancouver.

 **About Leonine Publishers**

Leonine Publishers LLC makes fine Catholic literature available to Catholics throughout the English-speaking world. Leonine Publishers offers an innovative "hybrid" approach to book publication that helps authors as well as readers. Please visit our web site to learn more about us. Browse our online bookstore to find more solid Catholic titles to uplift, challenge, and inspire.

Our patron and namesake is Pope Leo XIII, a prudent, yet uncompromising pope during the stormy years at the close of the 19th century. Please join us as we ask his intercession for our family of readers and authors.

www.leoninepublishers.com

www.ingramcontent.com/pod-product-compliance
Lightning Source LLC
Chambersburg PA
CBHW032357040426

42451CB00006B/39